ESSENTIALS OF THOUGHT LEADERSHIP & CONTENT MARKETING

BOOST YOUR BRAND, INCREASE YOUR MARKET SHARE, AND GENERATE QUALIFIED LEADS

Paul M. Kaplan

Fresno, California

Original illustrations by Robert Pizzo.

All adapted material reproduced by permission.

Published by Quill Driver Books
An imprint of Linden Publishing
2006 South Mary Street, Fresno, California 93721
(559) 233-6633 / (800) 345-4447
QuillDriverBooks.com

Quill Driver Books and Colophon are trademarks of
Linden Publishing, Inc.

ISBN 978-1-61035-316-8

135798642

Printed in the United States of America
on acid-free paper.

Library of Congress Cataloging-in-Publication Data on file.

For my twin brother, Andrew Kaplan, a communications professional at the U.S. Justice Department

Contents

Acknowledgments

I'd like to thank everyone I interviewed for this book, including Rob Leavitt at ITSMA, Tim Parker at the Bloom Group, Bonnie Kintzer, Rich Sutton at Trusted Media Brands Inc., and Amy Stein-Milford and Hanna Griff at the Museum at Eldridge Street. I also thank the research library staff at Harvard Business School, the faculty at the Yale School of Management, and Christine Kasman at the Yale Club library. I'm also grateful to these organizations for sharing their reports and decks for inclusion in this book.

A project as intensive as this is better served with the support of family and friends. I am thankful to my parents Jack and Eileen, brother Andrew Kaplan, uncle Ted Katz, and cousins Diane and Ed Ziegman, Robert and Jane Katz, David Allon, Daphne Balick, and Mango and Willow Ziegman. Thanks to Karen and Deha Rozanes–may this book serve as an inspiration to my nephews Kyle and Julian Rozanes when they start their careers in years to come.

I wish to also thank friends, including Barney Pearson, Jiyoung Cha, Jacob Koskimaki, Josh Brook, and Sharon Goldman for their support. I also am thankful for the encouragement of other friends: Christine Allers, Alfred Robert Hogan, Yan Ma, Sumesh Madan, Angela Pruitt, Karen Seiger, and Felix Kaplan. I thank Martha Soffer for her friendship and copy editing advice.

I also acknowledge the support from colleagues, professors, consultants, and managers at various jobs that I have held over the years for their insights and teaching in the digital marketing space.

Finally, many thanks to my publisher Kent Sorsky and publicity and marketing director Jaguar Bennett at Linden Publishing / Quill Driver Books for their advice and guidance throughout the process.

Introduction

Content marketing and thought leadership are terms that are frequently tossed around at companies, but often without defining them precisely or creating a rigorous system for producing and publicizing content marketing and measuring its results. Some books discuss how to create content marketing. Others are about marketing automation. Still others focus on customer relationship management tools. Few books put the pieces together.

That's where this book comes in. It connects the dots. To get the most out of it, though, I suggest that you read the book sequentially. Don't skip around or just read the chapter that seems most relevant. The book has a narrative. It begins by looking at how to develop a robust content marketing strategy. It shows how you can research your customers' needs and identify your company's areas of expertise. It then looks at how to bring this content to market through a variety of channels. These include email, social media, paid social media, and web marketing. It identifies best practices in developing a campaign landing page and explains how to draw in new users, as well as ways to pitch your most promising thought leadership to the media.

The book then examines how to turn campaign responders into leads through scoring, grading, and tracking them with campaign automation tools. Next it looks at ways to route leads to sales effectively and tools for sales enablement. Finally, the book suggests how to measure your results and report them to senior management.

Peppered throughout the book are primary interviews that I conducted with business leaders, thought leadership consulting companies, and business academics. I also interviewed business-to-business (American Express OPEN, IBM), consumer (Whole Foods), and nonprofit organizations (Museum at Eldridge Street) as mini-profiles for using content marketing.

In addition, there are visual representations of concepts throughout the chapters. These include models referenced, metric dashboards, infographics, survey findings from research companies, and screenshots.

I wrote this book for a wide audience, including marketers at consumer or business-to-business companies considering content marketing, as well as staff at agencies, consulting firms, and ad-tech firms, and freelance consultants advising their clients. The book is also relevant for entrepreneurs looking to grow their businesses. The content applies to both large and small for-profit and nonprofit organizations.

Visit my website at paulkaplanauthor.com to learn more and to leave comments.

Enjoy the book.

Section One

Developing a Thought Leadership and Content Strategy

1

What Content Marketing Can Do for You

In this chapter:

- What content marketing does—and what it can do for you
- Definition of content marketing and thought leadership
- How thought leadership educates buyers
- How thought leadership relates to the rest of your content marketing

Content and inbound marketing simultaneously solve three of every marketer's knottiest problems: generating leads, qualifying potential clients, and educating buyers about your products and services. Effective content marketing brings customers to you, because buyers self-select through their interest in the content you provide. Well-targeted content marketing screens out unqualified buyers by addressing the specific problems your company solves. Most important, content marketing educates buyers about the best solution for their needs—allowing you to influence how clients evaluate possible solutions.

The Content Marketing Institute defines content marketing as "a strategic marketing approach focused on creating and distributing valuable, relevant, and consistent content to attract and retain a clearly defined audience—and, ultimately, to drive profitable customer action."[1] This approach usually involves a long-term commitment to producing, sharing, promoting, and improving online materials that create prospect or customer interest in the company's products or services.

Importantly, content marketing, for the most part, does not try to promote the products themselves. The purpose is to build a company's brand and enlighten, educate, or entertain prospects and customers. Typically, companies use online channels such as social media, blogs, videos, games, polling, or interactive web pages. In some cases, companies conduct content marketing in their stores or at other events. The business goal is ultimately to increase customer acquisition, spend, and retention. Examples may be a recipe from a food store, advice from a tool manufacturer, or trends on retirement from a financial planner.

Thought leadership, the highest strategic level of content marketing

Thought leadership is a subsection of content marketing. At its best, thought leadership brings a fresh perspective to the marketplace on a particular issue. For example, it may explain the effect of a regulation or a market shift. Besides outlining the situation, excellent thought leadership will chart a course of action. It's not enough to define the problem or issue; thought leadership should guide the reader. The most helpful thought leadership also offers commercial insights so readers can see how to improve their businesses. Ultimately, the value of thought leadership is the value it brings to readers' organizations. Channels for thought leadership engagement usually include blogs, videos, social media, influencer blogs, tweets, pitches to media, and industry events and conferences.

> "Thought leadership consists of ideas that can lead people in unexpected directions. Thought leadership needs to be educational and ideally provocative."

Generally, thought leadership is more suited to business-to-business companies, though consumer companies can employ it when giving customers advice. An example would be a clothing brand writing a blog on how to accessorize outfits. In this case, that company sells such ware or partners with one that does. Thought leadership is more common and, in some ways, expected in business-to-business. An example would be an information service provider to building contractors relating the latest building trends and predicting their short- and medium-term impacts.

Jon Miller, vice president of product marketing at Marketo, notes that "both thought leadership and content marketing can very effectively build your awareness and brand, but . . . true thought leadership is much rarer. Thought leadership consists of ideas that require attention, that offer guidance or clarity and that can lead people in unexpected, sometimes contrarian directions. Thought leadership needs to be educational and ideally provocative; content marketing can simply be fun or entertaining."[2]

LinkedIn, a key platform for promoting thought leadership, offers its perspective as well: "Thought leadership is about sharing insights and ideas—and a unique point of view—that provoke new ways of thinking, spark discussions and debates, and inspire action. A true thought leader knows a topic inside and out, has formed a clear, unique and defensible point of view about it, and freely shares that perspective."[3]

As Jeff Ernst, principal analyst at Forrester Research, puts it: "Business buyers don't 'buy' your product or service, they 'buy into' your perspective and approach to solving their problems."[4]

How thought leadership can shape client thinking

The payoff for a company with a well-implemented thought leadership strategy is to elevate uncommitted buyers out of discussions about product minutia and to engage them at the strategic level. Studies show that companies value—even crave—a unique perspective from vendors. Respondents place a high value in breadth and depth of information as well as originality of thinking and ideas.

> Companies value—even crave—a unique perspective from vendors.

Another benefit of thought leadership is that it allows your company to better engage clients and prospects. Salespeople often say they need material to substantiate conversations, particularly in the beginning of relationships. Through a constant output of thought leadership, your company is less likely to be lost in the shuffle and more likely to be remembered at key purchase points. Business-to-business sales cycles are frequently long so this could be significant.

> Through a constant output of thought leadership, your company is more likely to be remembered at key purchase points.

Corporate Visions found that "74% of buyers choose the company that was first to add value as they are defining their buying vision."[5]

There are three steps for building a thought leadership marketing strategy:

1. Understand the current issues, evolving trends, and pressing business concerns for your prospects and clients.

2. Create a road map of how you think industry players should react to trends and problems.

3. Show how prospects and clients can solve some of these issues through your company's products or solutions. This does not mean simply showing them your sales collateral. Rather, you need to show—and customize—how your company's solutions can be a tool to solve for those specific issues and needs that plague your clients.

Marketers often miss the last point. Often, companies do not link their thought leadership to their clients' and prospects' business operations and needs. Unless marketers offer specific recommendations to improve business operations, clients cannot implement the findings of thought leadership. It is like giving them a forecast for a snowy day but not mentioning that they should wear snow boots, a scarf, and gloves.

Thought leadership must, in the end, introduce and map topics that address an audience's key issues and provide solutions for solving those issues. Put another way, marketers must ensure that there is "consistency in their company's mission and vision, what the company delivers in the market, and its marketing messages. This is key to making sure there's muscle behind getting your thought leadership noticed."[6]

Effective thought leadership leverages your company's unique knowledge to establish expertise

Bloom Group, a prominent thought leadership and content marketing consulting firm based in Boston, Massachusetts, defines thought leadership as "New, informative, useful information on a compelling, complex issue that positions a company or professional as an expert in a field."[7] Ultimately, thought leadership illuminates issues of interest to a particular industry. In the process, the company providing the thought leadership usually becomes better known and attracts more clients.

"Focus is absolutely key. The broader you go, the harder it is not to state the obvious."

In my interview with Tim Parker, partner at Bloom Group, he explained the importance of having content stand out in today's crowded marketplace. He noted Bloom Group's seven Hallmarks of Thought Leadership (see Table 1.1, page 7).

Parker also shared his thoughts on how a company without many resources can still hope to develop promising thought leadership. "Focus is absolutely key because you can often draw on field experience where you actually have unique insights, so you may not have to do much research to support your thesis. And if you do research, it too can be very focused. The broader you go,

	What Is It?	What We Do
Focus	Having a single, fundamental message	Clearly define issue/problem to research; create a theme statement/structure for the point of view (POV)
Novelty	Coming up with a unique diagnosis of the problem or solution	Conduct literature searches to review other POVs on topic and position for "white space"
Relevance	Meeting a critical and specific market need (making a case for action)	Gather evidence on prevalence and importance of problem through survey, case interviews, and literature surveys
Validity	Proving that the solution you offer is effective	From client work and analysis of best practice case studies, collect examples of companies that have followed the solution you prescribe
Practicality	Demonstrating you have a solution that can be implemented	Develop tools, frameworks, and methodologies that companies can use to solve the problem
Rigor	Having tight, consistent logic	Produce an early white paper that sets down the message, arguments, and evidence; test core frameworks and methods with internal group
Clarity	Making a clear argument, with words and concept	Identify and eliminate jargon, unclear concepts, and other confusing material from the POV

Table 1.1 Bloom Group's Hallmarks of Thought Leadership.

"Thought leadership has become the new competitive battleground for any B2B firm that competes on the basis of expertise and advice."[8]

the harder it is not to state the obvious. If you are a large organization with a sizable budget like McKinsey, you can spend the money doing original research—thereby saying something new about a big topic. But you need significant resources to do that."

When asked which companies are doing some of the best work in thought leadership and content marketing, Parker was quick to mention McKinsey and Boston Consulting Group. He offered several reasons:

- They compete on their expertise alone, and they are the best at it.

- They started doing thought leadership marketing 50 years ago, so they have had a lot of practice.

- They have the processes and people in-house.

- Their culture rewards pushing the intellectual envelope—at the very least some get kudos for doing it. This stands in contrast to other consulting firms that, for instance, reward rerunning the same process at multiple clients. That is an equally valid model, but those firms have trouble producing good thought leadership.

How thought leadership relates to the rest of your content marketing

Now, let's relate this discussion of thought leadership to the broad topic of content marketing. Generally, content marketing is viewed more broadly as curating and distributing content with the goal of acquiring and engaging customers. Importantly, content marketing is relevant for both consumer and business-to-business (B2B) companies.

Figure 1.1 on page 9 from Forrester Research shows the inverse relationship between the amount of content and its impact on potential buyers. Thought leadership, loosely defined as original ideas to guide the industry, has the most potential to influence potential buyers. This is particularly true for "top-of-the-funnel" buyers just learning about a brand or product. They are researching the problem they are seeking to solve.

Yet producing this kind of content is resource-consuming. It requires original, rigorous research, writing, and editing. Therefore, it rests on top of the

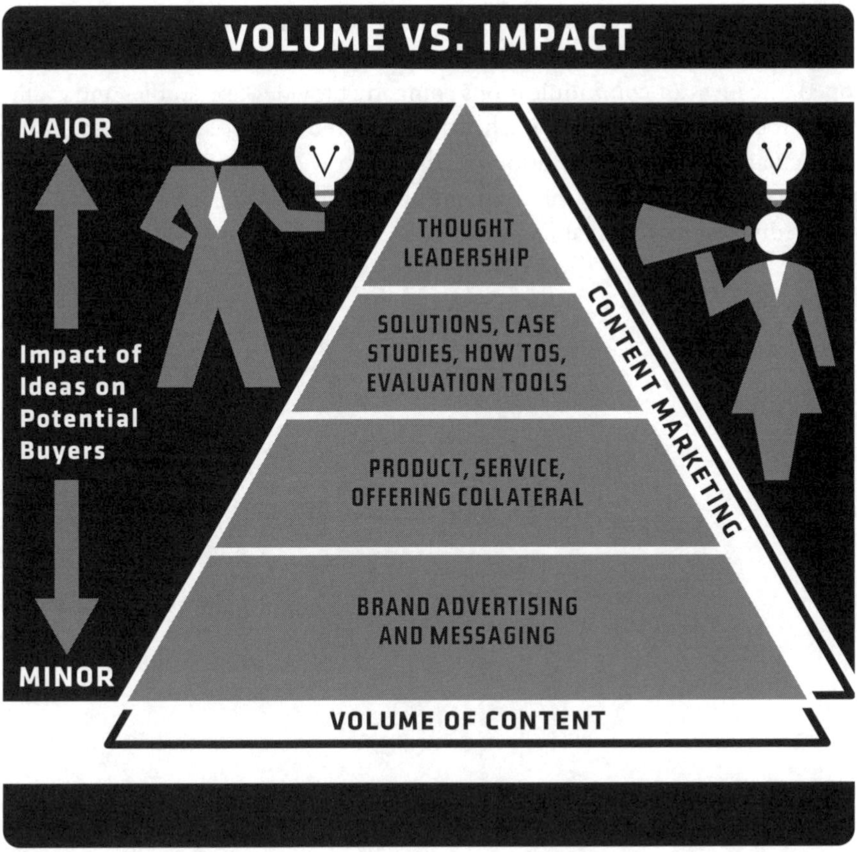

Figure 1.1 Volume of content versus impact on buyers. Illustration by Robert Pizzo; adapted from Forrester Research, "Nurture Thought Leadership to Nurture Your Brand," April 2013.

content marketing pyramid. Moving down the pyramid, the information is more "how-to" based. It guides the consumer. One level down is collateral for particular products and services underlying the solutions. Since this is not "objective" content, it carries less influence to the industry, but more marketing collateral is produced than thought leadership. At the bottom of the pyramid is brand advertising and messaging, which may play a vital role in promoting a company but rarely influence an industry.

An example is a multinational investor communications company that produces thought leadership on topics like how proxy statements can be digitized. This is an interesting idea for publicly traded companies that must issue proxies. Through this material, such companies come to know better the investor communications firm producing this content. As leads are developed, the investor communications company provides case studies and evaluation tools for its prospects, so that over time the warm leads learn about the particular products and solutions of the investor communications company. Throughout this process, the company's brand, advertising, sponsorships, and messaging reinforce its value.

2

Creating Your
Content Marketing Plan

In this chapter:

- Creating a content marketing strategy
- Aligning your content marketing to your company's marketing plan
- Business-to-business (B2B) vs. business-to-consumer (B2C) content marketing
- Identifying your company's areas of expertise
- Collecting and using existing content
- Defining your content marketing objectives

In this chapter, we'll discuss how to come up with a winning content strategy.

The first order of business is to create a global content marketing strategy. But there is a major step to take before writing that. The strategist needs to understand what marketing as a whole is trying to accomplish and how content will further these objectives. Otherwise, the content marketing program will have no real direction and won't align to overall business goals. It will lose internal support. Another danger is that output will be a series of one-off pieces that have little promotional value, audience appeal, or internal buy-in.

Overall marketing plan: The foundation

The first step is to read through the company's marketing strategy. Then gather the answers to these questions:

- What is the company's marketing objective?
- How does this objective contribute to revenue and profit?
- What are key customer segments?

- Are these segments translated into personas for other digital marketing efforts?

- What promotional tactics are currently used?

- Which tactics have been the most successful and why?

- What key metrics are used to measure success?

- Which products or solutions is the company emphasizing and why?

- What is the sales cycle?

Identifying company objectives that aren't in the marketing plan

If a marketing plan exists with the answers to these questions, great. But if not, you may have to do some digging.

Here are some suggestions:

- **Company objectives:** Examine sales goals by company, division, and region. You don't need to get too deep, but you should have the basics.

  Where to look: If your company is publicly traded, read the annual and quarterly reports carefully. Also read any analyst reports. If your company does "town halls," or employee meetings to discuss the company's trajectory, look through those presentations. If possible, obtain a copy of an internal sales report.

- **Marketing objectives:** How will marketing fulfill the overall company business objectives? Look for metrics like "increase leads by 10 percent" or "increase subscribers by 15 percent in fiscal year."

  Where to look: Ask the senior leadership in marketing. Review presentations on marketing strategy. Review company town hall meetings for statements about marketing objectives. Ask also about reviewing any marketing strategy presentations that were prepared for senior management.

- **Customer segments:** How does the company identify and define its key customer segments? Are they businesses or consumers? How are they distinguished? How does messaging vary among them? What are their needs?

  Where to look: Marketing town hall PowerPoint decks, presentations to senior management, any past consultant reports.

- **Competitive framework:** Who are the key competitors? The answer is often multifaceted, and you should primarily look at your company's competitors for specific products. Your business may have some partners for certain products who are competitors for other products.

  A competitor may compete with certain product lines but not others. For this purpose, you don't have to know the competition for every product your company has. Focus on the main competitors for the products that your marketing plan indicates you are trying to grow.

  Where to look: Look both within and outside your company for information. Start with the sales and marketing teams. You may need to conduct this search by country since competitors differ from location to location. Focus on the regions the marketing strategy emphasizes. Also look at analyst reports, though often their lists of competitors are inaccurate. Read industry reports. Market research reports often provide excellent analyses of competitors. You may have to pay for them so ask for a preview to see if the report is worth the cost.

- **Products prioritization:** Which products or services is the company trying to push the most? Do different units of the company prioritize different products?

  Where to look: Try the various business units' yearly and quarterly plans, sales plans, and town hall decks, as well as announcements to analysts if your company is public.

Once you have gathered this information, you will use it to build your content marketing plan. It will serve as your guide on what content to use, the intended audiences, and the business reasoning behind the project. In later chapters, we'll explore how to measure success and garner leads.

Think of the content plan as the house you are building. The marketing plan described above is the foundation. If you don't have the foundation right or simply skip it altogether, your house will be on shaky ground. Your content marketing may be short-lived.

Now let's turn to building the content marketing plan.

Content marketing plan: Identifying content topics

Your content marketing plan should define your major objectives and strategies but be succinct—as a rule, no more than five pages.

The first and most essential item in your plan is to define what editorial topics you will cover in your content marketing. This is key because in many ways what you choose as content will showcase the company's brand. Ultimately, the topics you choose should bring together client interests and needs with what your company has expertise in.

Start with the needs of your industry. What are the key trends and issues? What are your clients or customers struggling with? Think about any conferences you attended about this industry. What were key topics? What questions came up a lot from the audience? Read trade periodicals and notice what topics reemerge. What are the pain points of the industry you are serving?

> Start with the needs of your industry. What are your clients or customers struggling with?

Find out who are the key influencers in your industry and visit their blogs. Sites like Followerwonk and AllTop will allow you to identify and engage with them. Read their blogs and consider leaving comments. As you conduct this research, you can benefit by promoting your company in this space. Figure 2.1 (below) illustrates the various kinds of influencers.

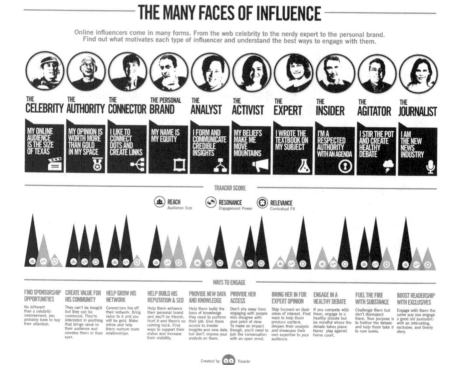

Figure 2.1 Different types of influencers. Courtesy of Smartinsights.com blog.

Make a list of at least five influencers in each major part of your business. For example, if your company has three major lines of business, try to find five influencers for each of the three. The distinction is important because influencers are often specific to a particular field. Write down their perspectives on industry issues. What topics do they bring up? How do they propose to solve for them, if at all? Themes will emerge. This will be crucial in building a content platform, which we will discuss later in the chapter.

Social media is also a primary vehicle for identifying influencers, trends, and issues for your industry. Which channels you choose will depend on whether you are a consumer or business-to-business marketer. For the latter, the most important channel will be LinkedIn, which is designed for this purpose. You will also want to review Twitter, YouTube, and Facebook, at a minimum, for content ideas. Let's discuss how to leverage each of these channels for the business-to-business marketer looking for content ideas. Afterward, we'll look at additional channels for the consumer marketer also in pursuit of content.

> Social media is a primary vehicle for identifying influencers, trends, and issues.

Identifying content topics for B2B markets

LinkedIn

Follow the influencers you found on LinkedIn. Read through their profile posts and notice the recurring themes. View what LinkedIn groups they are in and join those you deem most relevant. You may have to apply to some groups for entrance. If so, state your case to the administrator and what you can bring to the group.

Try to become a member of about five robust, lively, topical, and well-attended groups. A higher number will be difficult to manage if you are serious about consistently participating. Your objective in joining is to see which topics are resonating with users. When you are at the stage of promoting your content, these groups will play a crucial role. We'll discuss that later.

Ask the following questions to select the best groups:

- Is the group active? How many posts occur each day and week?
- Is the discussion about topics related to my industry?
- Is there a sizable user base? (A small user group is OK for niche topics.)

- Is much of the discussion about job opportunities or vendors pitching their products?

- Do users ask and answer questions among one another or is the group messaging a lot of one-off posts with virtually no comments?

Remember, less is more. Don't spread yourself too thin by entering too many groups and then not participating. Choose a few and apply to them if needed. Feel free to post questions to the groups about key issues or trends that they think are important or that their companies are struggling with. After reading through posts and group messages on LinkedIn, jot down additional ideas for content areas.

Twitter

On Twitter, your challenge will be finding the pertinent information amid lots of noise. Start with finding which hashtags are used in your industry on Twitter. Notice who is tweeting substantive information on topics, their followership, and their influence in social media. By clicking on users' profile pages, you can see their followership.

At this point, you are trying to accomplish two crucial tasks. The first is to identify key issues for content. The second task is often overlooked but equally important. You are networking among influencers. You want to listen, respond intelligently, and get your company's name in the conversation. You are lining up contacts to whom you will promote your content. In the ecosystem of social media, your aim will be for these influencers to retweet, blog, and link to your content. We'll discuss this further later in the chapter.

If your business does not already have a Twitter account, see if you can start one. Ask your corporate communications department if this is possible. If your company already has one, ask if you can tweet replies, direct messages, and retweet. The key point is entering the conversation.

Let's look at each technique:

- **Direct message (DM)** replies are private messages to the Twitter user. Your company's followers will not see them. This is effective for a one-on-one conversation. You may want to direct-message a content creator with any interesting points, comments, or questions. You can also thank the content creator if you found a particular article or infographic helpful. Later, we will discuss promotion of content and how contacts with content creators will prove useful.

- **Retweeting** is your company tweeting someone else's message to your followers. It's a way of amplifying the original poster's message. It's also a way for an influencer to take notice of your company's Twitter handle after you have retweeted consistently. You can add your own messaging to the retweet, though character limitations may prevent writing much.

- **List building** is an important way to cut through the clutter of Twitter. Go to Hootsuite and enter the Twitter handles of the people who write about the topics you're interested in and who have a sizable followership. To create this list, you will have to peruse through many tweets to decide which users are most relevant. Much of it will be noise—a myriad of press releases, irrelevant product information, and unrelated information. Think of your list as a trusted source for carving out the most relevant ideas for building your editorial content.

YouTube and Facebook

YouTube is also crucial. Search for any videos of influencers you found on the other channels. View videos from conferences in your industry. As you visit the YouTube channels, observe how they're organized. In which subject areas are videos grouped? Are they grouped by themes? Which videos received the most views?

Also make sure to visit the Facebook profiles of users or companies with stellar content, though many business-to-business marketers tend to overlook Facebook, relegating it to the consumer realm. But many industry leaders post links to some very engaging articles, points of view, and blogs here. Many of these links will direct back to their websites, which contain rich sources of information.

Don't rely solely on social media

Besides social media, you'll want to look at any market research that your company has done about your clients' interests. Watch videos or read through reports of any focus groups completed in the past few years. Surveys providing quantitative and statistically significant information are also very helpful if your company has done them.

Informally interview some of the front-line sales leaders. Based on their client and prospect interactions, what have they found to be the most pressing issues? To borrow a cliché, "What keeps their clients up at night?"

On the other side of the coin, on what topics do salespeople want content to drive the conversation with clients and prospects? Part of the reason for

> Part of the reason for content marketing is to position salespeople as problem solvers and industry experts.

content marketing is to position salespeople as problem solvers and industry experts rather than just product pushers. After all, clients are paying for expertise.

I recommend that you choose two or three sales leaders and ask them these questions in a 20-minute meeting. Just mentioning it to them in the hallway or emailing them questions may not get a positive response. Moreover, you want to ensure that the answers are structured and not haphazard.

Identifying content topics for consumer markets

Your job here is to create content that will educate, wow, enlighten, and drive consumers within your industry. You must find out the needs of your customers: What information are they looking for? Why are they seeking it? For example, if you're a travel company, you probably know that consumers are looking for deals. But that's limited to transactions. With content, you want to go deeper. What information do customers have about travel planning? Some may ask why they would need a travel agent at all in the digital age. Still others may want to get the best recommendations on travel sites, lodging, and eateries to try.

These consumer needs lend themselves to great content ideas. Continuing with the travel agency example, a suitable article may be "How to plan a multigenerational trip" or "How to best work with a travel agent" or "When booking trips on the Internet will not cut it." These topics address customer questions. They also align with the specific areas of expertise for a travel agency. If all the articles were about tourist sites to visit in Budapest, Hungary, the content would be competing with travel guides, books, and articles. The way to handle this is to curate content, which we will discuss later in the chapter.

> In a commodity space, content differentiates a company as a problem solver.

Importantly, this content differentiates the travel agency within the industry. In a commodity-oriented space, the agency can stand out as a problem solver. It positions the agency as providing counsel rather than merely booking trips. After all, that is one of the reasons a customer would visit a travel agent rather than simply booking on an online site.

The travel agency is one example. Any consumer product or service can develop and leverage relevant, robust, and consistent content. We'll discuss how to promote it in a later chapter.

Use listening tools to identify customer needs

Social media can be a highly useful source for gathering information about consumers' needs and preferences. I recommend your company invest in a listening tool to methodically collect this information. A good listening tool will aggregate social media entries grouped by your search terms, allowing you to understand what your customers, prospects, and competitors think about various aspects of your business or any other topic. You may ask, why not just do Google searches and set Google alerts? If your budget is very tight, free Google tools may be your best option. But if your budget can afford one, a listening tool will pick up what users are communicating in a more stream-lined and consistent fashion than the free tools will.

If you choose this path, I recommend that you ask the vendor for a free trial for a month so you can test it out. One of the hardest parts is selecting keywords. You will want to make sure you are entering keywords that your customers actually use. Listening tools aren't just for generating content ideas—you can also leverage them to systematically view what customers are saying about your brand, products, competitors, and industry.

Identifying your company's expertise

Now you have a host of ideas of what your customers' and industries' content needs are. Let's turn to the other side of the coin. What subject matter expertise does your company have to meet these needs?

I recommend that you conduct an internal audit of thought leaders. Start by viewing any industry conferences where your company's managers have presented. Look for videos or decks of these talks or panels that you can screen or review.

For other leads of internal resources, ask your communications department as well as sales or product teams. If your company uses a public relations firm, inquire for recommendations on thought leaders within the enterprise.

The key questions are:

- What are the company's areas of expertise?

- What does the company want to be seen as an expert in?

- Who in the company can provide this?

If you are an agency or consultant helping your client, you may be at a disadvantage in that you will not know many of the people. Ask your client contact to provide you with a list of possible internal thought leaders to interview.

Thought leaders don't always know they are thought leaders

Many potential subject matter experts at your or your client's company may not be used to seeing themselves as thought leaders. They may even respond, "I'm not an expert in that." But they may not realize they are. If they have been doing a certain kind of work for many years, understand the larger industry implications of their work, and can speak articulately about it, they may be whom you are seeking.

Another benefit of using internal subject matter experts is wider exposure for the company. To accomplish this, make sure your subject matter experts' online presence is relevant and updated. You would be surprised how key employees have a half-baked LinkedIn profile or no other substantive online domain. We'll discuss in a later chapter how to enhance these properties for subject matter experts or key salespeople.

Creating a thought leadership platform

Now you are ready to create your thought leadership platform. Ask the following questions:

- What are the top five subjects for thought leadership?

- Are these areas distinct? Are they broad enough to be categories yet still focused?

- Are these subjects mere trends and likely to be unimportant in a few years or are they likely to be important for at least several years?

- Are there subject matter experts at your company who can speak or write about these issues?

It's OK to use outside experts—but you still need to add value

Importantly, you don't have to have subject matter experts within your company to cover a topic in your content marketing. You can look for this knowledge in partners, select vendors, or outside consultants. But the use of outside experts is not without a price. Your company will not get knowledge equity from white papers written by outsiders or YouTube videos made by consultants.

Knowledge equity is the industry recognizing your company as the originator of a particular idea, trend, insight, or phrase. One of the goals of your content marketing should be for your company to receive credit for its contributions to thought leadership. This is especially important if your product is based on your company's industry expertise or you offer consulting services for your clients. Your firm's knowledge equity helps justify why a prospect should choose your company over competitors, because it proves why your company is more knowledgeable and can guide clients better. Without knowledge equity, information is being distributed to the industry, but your firm is not getting any credit for it.

The solution is to cobrand content with partners. Think of other companies that may have content experts who can contribute material. You have to think of what your company will bring to the table in this cobranding arrangement. It could be a strong brand, money to pay for production of materials, or promotion strength.

Reuse content in many forms

Another important consideration is scalability. You want to create content that you will be able to refurbish in different formats. If you go through the trouble of writing a white paper outlining key issues with charts and figures, you should reuse this material for other applicable formats. You may create a few short videos for your company's YouTube channel on this topic. You may also want to create an infographic from the material or a shorter deck for SlideShare.

Defining subject areas and topics

When you have identified your five subject areas, the next step is to compile examples of topics within each area. Write a list of at least five topics for a total of 25. (Note that smaller companies may want to start with fewer.) Then for each topic, consider what your formats will be and who the subject matter experts will be. It should align with the objectives of the overall marketing plan we reviewed

Your topics, formats, and experts should align with the objectives of the overall marketing plan.

earlier. This will form the basis of your content marketing plan. (See Figure 2.2 on page 22 for an example of a topic framework.)

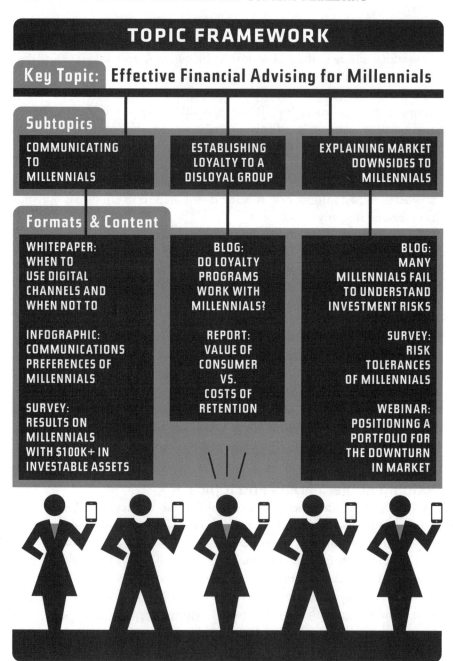

Figure 2.2 Example of a topic framework. Illustration by Robert Pizzo.

Curating content

So far, we have covered the creation of original material. You can also use curated content, meaning repurposed existing material. There is excellent content that you can promote through your channels, which we will discuss in a later chapter. At least two-thirds of your content should be original, the other third curated. If you go over that ratio, your content will appear unoriginal. That said, curating is an effective way to increase your flow of content.

> At least two-thirds of your content should be original—under that, you'll appear derivative.

Cite your sources

Curation does, however, come with a few pitfalls to avoid. First and foremost, it is essential to credit any chart or other visual or original quote you use. You can do this through a courtesy line for the asset you are using. For original quotes, consider using an endnote to give credit to the company that created the quotation. You can also have a sources section. It's a fine balance. You want to cite properly, but you also don't want your work to be overly academic. In some cases, you will need to ask permission from companies before using their assets. If you would like to use proprietary data or an original diagram in your white paper, deck, or video, you should ask the company that created it for permission to do so. Speak to your legal team about any contract that would need to be signed. In some cases, the company or creator of the asset may ask for compensation. That's usually negotiable.

Find content by linking to trusted sources

An easier and more common way to curate content is simply through linking to preexisting content. On your social media platforms, you can create a list of *trusted sources*. These are both individuals and companies you believe would make valuable contributions that you would like to share. These sources are also known to have accurate and reliable information. It's important to filter out the noise and plethora of inaccurate, overly salesy, or biased sources.

I recommend that you build your list in a few ways. First, ask your communications department and businesses what sources they use. Review the Twitter, LinkedIn, and Facebook pages of those they recommend. What percentage of these sources' content is original? Is their content relevant for your audience? Are these sources considered authorities in this field? Who is following and commenting on their sites—and should these commenters be included on your list?

Several times a week you should go to these social media pages and share the best and most pertinent comments with your followers. You are trying to accomplish several items here:

1. You want to expand your editorial offerings with high-quality, relevant curated content.

2. You want to inform your followers about this excellent content that they likely would not find on their own.

3. You want to establish your company's value in the industry as a thought leader.

You want to increase your site's search engine optimization (SEO). The more you establish these relationships and share content, the easier it will be to acquire backlinks from these high-trafficked domains you are visiting and sending users to. Establishing backlinks is a key part of SEO enhancement. We will discuss SEO more in chapter 17, "Organic Search Results."

Content marketing plan: Objectives and justification

Let's recap where we are and what needs to come next. You have the overall marketing plan and objectives. You now also have robust, well-supported ideas for content categories as well as topics for each. You know the format you want to try and how to scale one larger piece of content into different kinds of formats for various user segments with varying needs.

The missing piece is connecting your marketing plan to your content. What are you trying to achieve with your content and how? Think of the grand marketing plan we discussed earlier in the chapter as the highest level and the content topics as the way to communicate them. You need to link the two.

Explain your objectives for doing content. How would you measure these?

Explain your objectives for doing content. Do you want to increase brand awareness? Enhance your company's influence? Generate leads? If you want to accomplish more than one objective, rank them in importance.

How would you measure these objectives? Has your company done any brand awareness or media perception studies where you can compare pre- and post-content execution? For lead generation, how are you defining a lead? It may be difficult at this stage for you to quantify a goal of how many leads.

But you can put a stake in the ground. At the very least, your plan should describe the process of lead generation, including how you will capture leads, score them, and promote to them. We'll discuss those facets in subsequent chapters.

You can also spell out the quantity of content you are planning and its intended effect. For example, "Through three white papers and associated videos per quarter, I will grow net new leads by 20 percent."

Remember this quote: "The benefit of content marketing for your company must be quantified and linked to your management's marketing metrics in order for content to get a seat at the table."

Your plan should also address targeting. Think in terms of customer segments. Which customer segments are you reaching with each topic? Who are they? What do you know about their needs? We'll discuss this later when we look at "business types" or "personas."

Achieving content marketing is tricky. Few may be aware of it. Even fewer know of its benefits. You will need to sell content marketing to your or your client's management and likely sales team. We'll discuss how to do this effectively in chapter 23, "Communicating to Senior Management."

Now that you have your content marketing plan, let's look at how to put it into action.

3

Evaluating and Reusing Existing Content

In this chapter:

- Identifying existing content you can reuse
- Evaluating existing content for quality and alignment with business strategy
- Identifying topics that require new content
- Tips for updating old content

In the last chapter, we discussed how to create your content marketing plan. This plan sets forth your objectives, how you intend to get there, and the value your objectives will bring to your company.

Now, let's turn to the nuts and bolts of producing the content.

Auditing your existing content

The first step is to audit your current content. You may find that your company has produced multiple content pieces, but they are not categorized, indexed, or even in one place. Because of turnover at your company over the years, there may be some terrific pieces that few current employees know about. Still others may be outdated yet remain on your website.

There are a few reasons why this step is key. First, you don't want to reinvent the wheel. There's no need

> You don't want to reinvent the wheel. There's no need to create content that already exists within your company.

to create content that already exists within your company. You may want to update, tweak, or customize it, but that is far easier than creating it from scratch.

If your company has a content management system (CMS), you may be able to automatically aggregate content for your audit.

Kristina Halvorson and Melissa Rach's *Content Strategy for the Web* outlines three kinds of audit, as shown in Table 3.1:

Audit Type	Description	Stage to Employ
Inventory by the numbers	A list of all content by category just as a warehouse would catalog its inventory	As a first step in formulating your content strategy
Best practices assessment	A third-party assessment (or your own) of how your content stacks up against that of the competition and versus industry best practices	When refining your content strategy to ensure that it has a competitive advantage
Strategic assessment	An examination of how your company's content aligns with strategic management goals	After content is cataloged and before recommendations on content categories

Table 3.1 Three types of content audit. Reproduced from Kristina Halvorson and Melissa Rach's *Content Strategy for the Web* (Berkeley, CA: New Riders/Peachpit, 2012).

In your audit, you need to evaluate your content for many parameters. Here are some key questions:

- Categorize the content by the editorial topics that you chose. Make sure that you have content pieces in every appropriate format for each topic. Which topics are not covered in all formats?

- Note which content has been gated or requires actions from users such as giving their personal information to access. (For more information on gating content, see chapter 12, "Building a Campaign Landing Page.")

- Categorize your content by which pieces are associated with what part of the buyer's journey; for example, awareness, consideration, decision, or purchase.

- Identify which parts of your business each content piece is associated with.

- Identify content pieces that are outdated. A content piece is not necessarily out of date because of when it was created, but whether it references obsolete events or predictions. For example, a content piece may be outdated because it cites events in the "future" that have now already happened. Or it may warn against impending legislation that was never passed. A content piece may also cite studies that have since been updated.

- Identify which topics have received the most engagement, as defined by likes, shares, comments, click-throughs, and conversions. Your content management system may be able to generate this report. If not, your marketing automation tool may. Also, look at past dashboards that may have these metrics.

Table 3.2 below gives an example of the content audit for a financial services company targeting financial advisors and registered investment advisors:

Title	Format	Gated	Out of Date	Topic	Conversion
Communicating Investing Tools to Millennials	White-paper	Yes	No	Investor Communica-tions	20%
Effect of Regulation on Capital Markets	PowerPoint Deck	Yes	Yes	Regulation	15%
Best Practices in Accounting Reconciliation	Infographic Series	No	No	Operations Technology	NA (not gated)
How Investors Are Voting this Year	Data Report	Yes	Yes	Shareholder Voting	5%

Table 3.2 Example of a content audit.

What to do with your existing content

The point of this laborious exercise is to determine which topics need more content and which topics already have a fair amount of usable content that you don't need to recreate. Leveraging your existing content can save you considerable time in the long run. A content audit is also a must-seize opportunity to identify and retire outdated content.

As you audit your content, you should make a recommendation for each piece: delete, update, or merge.

Delete the piece if you feel the topic no longer has any relevance. If you delete obsolete pieces from your content management system, make sure the deletion doesn't leave broken links or error pages. This often happens when a piece is removed but you do not trace back all possible links. Such oversights will hinder your SEO scores as well as create negative user experiences.

Updating a content piece may take some resources so be sure that it is worth doing. Here are some key questions you should ask before committing to updating older content:

- Is the overall concept still viable and of interest to your target base?

- How much of the piece would need to be changed?

- Also, will your changes at some point need updating again? This is where your content management system will come in handy. Check if there is a scheduling and reminder function. You may need to revisit your content at a specified period in the future.

Merging may be a good option if you feel an older content piece still has validity but would now work better as a part of another piece. Even though the piece as a whole may be obsolete, parts of it may still be valuable as raw material for new content. An old content piece may contain charts, images, or statistics you would like to include in other pieces. Look at what kind of engagement the piece got when you first released it. If it resonated with readers but now has outdated content, think about how to repurpose the content by merging it into another piece.

4

Defining Your Audience

In this chapter:

- Defining your audience by personas
- Dividing your audience into segments
- Matching personas with appropriate content

The last chapter outlined ways you can audit and catalog your existing content. Your content audit will tell you which subjects have already been covered and which will need new material.

The next step is to define the audience for your content. When deciding what content you want to produce, you should have a distinct audience in mind. Who is the target audience? Who would be most interested in this material?

Above all, ask yourself: How does the content you are producing answer your clients' and prospects' needs?

Of course, different clients have different needs, so you'll want to divide your audience into segments according to their needs and interests. Each audience segment can be defined by a profile of a typical client called a *persona*. Personas can be defined by demographics, psychographics, company role, industry, or any other factor that affects clients' buying decisions.

> Above all, ask yourself how your content answers your clients' needs.

Identifying personas

The first step in defining your audience is to identify personas for your content. Personas should be specific, so you will likely need to use different personas for each of your product groups. For example, if you are marketing technology solutions to financial services companies, one persona you might use is "technology officer at global financial services company." If you also sell a solution for banks complying with new regulations, you may need to address a different persona—even if you're marketing to the same company.

Defining personas and matching them to appropriate content is useful for marketing to both consumers and business-to-business clients.

On the consumer side, for example, a financial advisory firm might market to these personas:

- Retiree looking for advice on fixed-income products
- Widow needing consultation on estate distribution
- Newly married couple looking to share resources
- Millennial starting to save and hoping to buy a house in one to four years

For a business-to-business example, let's suppose you are selling recruiting solutions. You might market to personas such as:

- Human resources recruiting managers at companies with 5,000+ employees
- Recruiting managers at companies with 500–5,000 employees
- Human resources directors at companies with 50–500 employees
- Headhunters or external recruiters

These four personas are defined by company size because your solutions vary by company size. Absent from the list are companies with fewer than 50 employees, because your management does not consider companies that small to be a target. The personas listed are also defined by job titles. For larger companies, the persona is the recruiting manager whereas for companies with 50–500 employees, the persona is at the director level. This group of personas also distinguishes between internal employees (human resources recruiting professionals) and external employees (recruiters at vendor firms).

Differences matter. Create different content to address specific needs.

The point of this list is that these differences matter. You may have different solutions for each of these personas. And you should create or adapt different versions of your content to address their specific needs.

Whether consumer or business-to-business, the trick is to come up with a manageable number of personas that you can act on. As a rough range, you may have 5 to 15 personas, depending on your global reach and product complexity. Less is more. Don't create any more personas than you need.

Ask these questions to narrow down your list:

- Are the personas distinct?

- Is each persona connected directly with a product type?

- Is this persona and/or associated product type crucial for your business?

- Do you have or could you create sufficient content for each persona?

Note that you don't have to create unique content for each persona. Instead, you can often tailor a content piece for various personas. You may also promote them differently. Let's go back to the example of the financial advisory firm. If you have created a white paper about effective financial advisor communication to clients, there could be four versions for each persona. Most of the content could be the same, but each version would go into more depth about that demographic.

The promotion of the white paper would also vary by persona. For example, you may try different LinkedIn groups that focus on these topics. Or you may try different hashtags on Twitter or utilize different keywords on a Google paid search.

Once you have identified personas appropriate for your business, look at them against your content audit. Determine which content belongs to which personas. You can then identify what gaps you have. In the next chapter, we'll discuss stages in the buyer's journey that can also be incorporated into your analysis. The goal is to identify which personas are lacking content at which stages of the buyer's journey.

5

Mapping Your Content
to the Buyer's Journey

In this chapter:

- The buyer's journey
- Understanding clients' concerns
- Defining content for each stage in the buyer's journey

So far, we have discussed ways you can define customer personas and match them against your content audit. This allows you to map where you need more content.

In this chapter, we'll take our analysis one step further by looking at how to identify persona needs at each stage of the buyer's journey.

The classic buyer's journey, which will be referenced throughout this book, is a map of the customer's decision points while evaluating and choosing a product. Figure 5.1 on page 36 illustrates two types of buyer's journey: business-to-business, which usually involves more decision points and longer, more complex sales cycles; and consumer, which is typically simple and more direct.

Three client concerns that drive the buyer's journey

The buyer's journey is defined by three client questions:

- **What** are the key problems that I am trying to solve?
- **How** will I do this?
- **Who** can help me do this?

Figure 5.2 on page 37 shows these three different stages of the journey and how to map content around it.

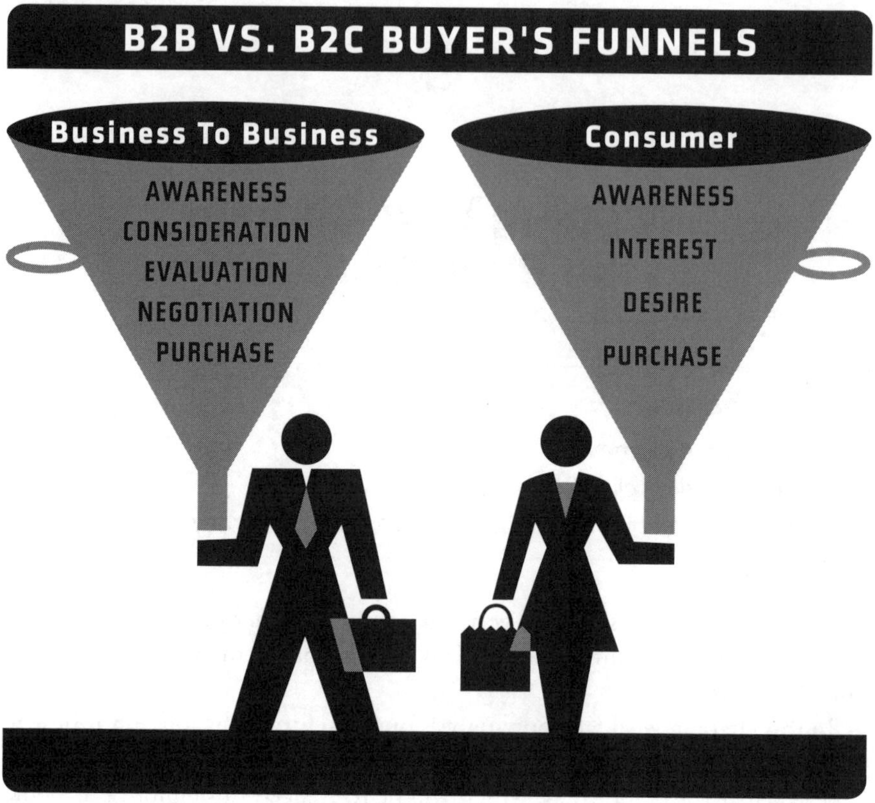

B2B VS. B2C BUYER'S FUNNELS

Business To Business

AWARENESS
CONSIDERATION
EVALUATION
NEGOTIATION
PURCHASE

Consumer

AWARENESS
INTEREST
DESIRE
PURCHASE

Figure 5.1 Business to business versus consumer buyer's funnels. Illustration by Robert Pizzo.

Defining content for each stage of the buyer's journey

The "What"

The "What" will be the bulk of your content. It's the beginning of the buyer's journey. You are introducing issues, trends, and data about your industry. In the process, you are seeking to increase your firm's brand awareness and standing in the industry.

Here are some types of content that answer "What" questions:

Blogs: A few hundred words explaining a particular issue of concern to your industry. A good blog is focused and presents a point of view. A blog should be updated frequently, so starting a blog entails a commitment by your organization. Since blogs are shorter-form content, they are usually ungated, but you can encourage readers to subscribe for additional content.

Figure 5.2 Mapping content to the buyer's journey. Illustration by Robert Pizzo.

More importantly, by having highly trafficked third-party sites link to your blog, you can substantially increase your search engine optimization. (For more information, see chapter 11, "Blogging.")

Market data: If your firm produces reports with proprietary data that you are willing to share, market data makes for prime content. Market data can take many forms. It can be surveys of panels or market trend data. The most valuable data is proprietary. It's possible that your firm has gathered such data in the course of doing business but has never thought about it as "content." One example is a retailer that tracks sales by categories. This information might be valuable to prospective clients, and it's exclusive data that no one else has. Experts within your firm may have used this data to develop insights or perspective on the market, which is also valuable information. When using market data, you should be careful to maintain customer privacy. All data should be reported in the aggregate to avoid any privacy issues.

You may want to sell market data or make it available only to clients. One recommendation is to give away a sample of the data but reserve the heart of the information for clients. However, if the information has very high public relations value (see chapter 9, "Public Relations"), it may be worth making all of it available. In other words, the expected revenues from selling the information may be less than the expected increase in sales from favorable public relations.

White papers: These have fallen out of fashion in large part, but they still can play an important role. In white papers, you outline an issue, provide examples, examine solutions, and present alternatives. White papers or long-form content is appropriate for readers who need in-depth and carefully researched information. For them, blogs and short and pretty decks are superficial. Since members of this audience are likely to be major players in the industry, they are probably already familiar with many of these topics. But the advantage of a white paper is that it goes deeper and provides greater insight than short-form content. Long, in-depth content doesn't have to be boring—there are ways to make white papers more inviting. Use text boxes to summarize points, bullets, images, and artwork. Catchy titles help too.

Infographics: The best infographics do more than report data. They tell the story behind the data by showing the connection between isolated data points. They show visually how one data point relates to another—and what this means for the outcome. Work with your graphic artist on creating infographics or outsource them to a firm specializing in them. Infographics are perfect for social media, especially LinkedIn, because they're likely to get shared.

The "How"

"How" content is for audiences in the middle of the buyer's journey. These potential clients have identified their problems and are now looking for solutions. "How" content can be some of your most valuable tools for educating your customers on how to evaluate possible solutions and avoid mistakes. This content describes methods and general approaches and outlines their advantages and disadvantages.

Typical formats for "How" content include:

Guides: These short reports are meant to be practical tips for the reader to implement. Guides should try to answer key reader questions like "How can I grow my business?" or "How can I avoid costly litigation?" A guide can also challenge conventional thinking. For example, building product manufacturers may think architects are not interested in their products if they have not specified them or put their brands in the requirements documents. Yet research shows that in certain cases architects are open to considering other products. This reveals a key opportunity for manufacturers. So a guide for building product manufacturers could explain this opportunity, then outline several ways that building product manufacturers can market more effectively to architects. The emphasis in a guide is tactics rather than strategy, but statistics and anecdotes can be employed to make the case.

Tip sheets: While guides tend to be longer and more elaborate, tip sheets offer quick, easy-to-read suggestions. They should focus on one area for your client so they are not too generic. Tip sheets can also have links to helpful directories, sites, and industry information. You should vet these sites very carefully, though, before recommending them. Tip sheets are often good for smaller clients or consumers who will be reading your content quickly, on the go, and want bite-size information.

Webinars: These are interactive ways to express the same kind of information you would include in guides and tip sheets. You can adapt a guide to create a webinar. Webinar deck slides don't need to have a lot of text, because their purpose is to illustrate concepts. The important element is the script for the moderator, which outlines what is to be said for each slide. You will want to find an internal expert to host the webinar. He or she should be someone who knows the subject and is also somewhat media savvy. Excellent presentation skills are paramount. Selecting a webinar moderator also provides a chance to showcase your company's thought leaders. Webinars should always give attendees a chance to ask questions. Many platforms allow participants to type in a question and the moderator to select which questions to answer.

Another best practice with webinars is to poll participants during the event. You can ask if they would like more information or to be contacted on how to implement some of what they learned. Attendees who answer yes become the "hot leads." This is important if you are going to segment webinar attendees. For example, you may want to separate out those who registered but did not attend, those who attended but said they did not want further information, and those who attended but did express an interest in more information about the company. You should also email registrants who did not attend with a link to watch the webinar on demand.

The "Who"

Importantly, this category is not thought leadership. It is not an "objective" account of the industry. Instead, "Who" content explains why your company is the right choice. It is essential that you separate this category and not mix it with thought leadership. Label it differently. If you don't do this, the distinction between objective analysis and marketing will be blurred. And your thought leadership will lose credibility in the marketplace for not being objective.

"Who" content can include:

Case studies: These are the clients' point of view on your company. A good practice is to ask your sales team to point out clients who are particularly happy with your products, services, or account support. If your company has multiple customer segments, strive to collect case studies in different segments. When you approach clients, tell them what you are looking to do and what you expect to do with the case study. You should have your legal department draft a release.

The idea behind a case study is that it goes in-depth. It's not just a few quotes. Rather, it explores the clients' business challenge and how your company's products solved them. Case studies can vary in length but are usually around three to five pages. Case studies are persuasive because they prove that your product solves real-world problems, and detailed information about your client make case studies even more realistic and persuasive. Here are some of the details you should include in case studies:

- Text boxes of pull quotes from clients

- Callouts of products the clients use

- Background on client's business

- Artwork

- Client's logo

- Photo of client

Be careful to:

- Ask clients if you can use the photos on their website.

- *Always* give clients final editing rights and ensure that they are comfortable with everything before you use the case studies.

Product demos: Webinars are not just for thought leadership. You can demonstrate how to use a product and why it will help a client in a webinar. Product demos can be used for prospects, but they're more effective as an engagement tool for clients. It is likely that your clients are underutilizing your products and services—most consumers and businesses do. So make sure your product demo has substance. It should not just be touting the benefits of the products. Show how to make the best use of your product or leverage its unique features. Offer tips. The demo's underlying theme can be "Are you making the most of this product? There may be helpful features with it that you are not aware of." Give participants a chance to ask questions. Follow up with participants who don't get to ask questions.

6

Best Practices
in Content Development

In this chapter:

- What buyers want from content providers
- Content development tips from top marketers

Now let's go deeper into what makes stellar content marketing. To gain an empirical understanding of what buyers are looking for from content marketing, we'll now turn to a study from ITSMA, a research company based in Lexington, Massachusetts.

Personalization

In a survey of global B2B buyers, ITSMA found that 60 percent of buyers perceive personalization as "valuable or very valuable" while just 11 percent "fail to see value or find it annoying."[1] (See Figure 6.1 below.)

Figure 6.1 ITSMA Global Buyer Survey responses. Up to five responses allowed. Reproduced from ITSMA How B2B Buyers Consume Information Survey, 2016.

Objectivity

Unsurprisingly, the most important thing to buyers is content that is relevant, unbiased, and not a sales pitch. In-depth understanding of the industry and clients' unique business needs is paramount. An important finding is that buyers also want "quantifiable value of the proposed solution." This underscores the importance of commercial insight in thought leadership. Your content should ultimately provide users with information and tips that will help them grow their business.

> The most important thing to buyers is content that is unbiased.

Quality content is vital before *and* after a sale

The ITSMA survey also showed that 81 percent of buyers "view content, especially thought leadership, as critical or important during the early stages of the buying process."[2] (See Figures 6.2 and 6.3.) Educating and influencing prospects early in the buyer's journey is critical. (For more on the buyer's journey, see chapter 5, "Mapping Your Content to the Buyer's Journey.")

Needs for content differ by the buyer stage. For initial research, peer reviews, case studies, "how-to" information, and best practices are paramount.

Importance of thought leadership

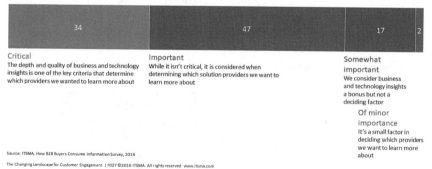

When you were doing your initial solution research for your most recent solution, what role did the solution providers' content such as research, analysis, and advice often found in reports, presentations, webcasts, videos, and articles, play in determining which providers you wanted to learn more about? % of respondents (N=402)

| 34 | 47 | 17 | 2 |

Critical
The depth and quality of business and technology insights is one of the key criteria that determine which providers we wanted to learn more about

Important
While it isn't critical, it is considered when determining which solution providers we want to learn more about

Somewhat important
We consider business and technology insights a bonus but not a deciding factor

Of minor importance
It's a small factor in deciding which providers we want to learn more about

Source: ITSMA, How B2B Buyers Consume Information Survey, 2016

The Changing Landscape for Customer Engagement | F027 ©2016 ITSMA. All rights reserved www.itsma.com

Figure 6.2 Importance of thought leadership to buyers. Reproduced from ITSMA How B2B Buyers Consume Information Survey, 2016.

Initial research: types of information needed

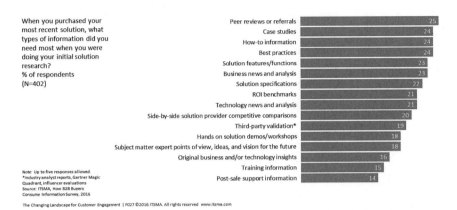

When you purchased your most recent solution, what types of information did you need most when you were doing your initial solution research?
% of respondents
(N=402)

Peer reviews or referrals — 25
Case studies — 24
How-to information — 24
Best practices — 24
Solution features/functions — 23
Business news and analysis — 23
Solution specifications — 22
ROI benchmarks — 21
Technology news and analysis — 21
Side-by-side solution provider competitive comparisons — 20
Third-party validation* — 19
Hands on solution demos/workshops — 18
Subject matter expert points of view, ideas, and vision for the future — 18
Original business and/or technology insights — 16
Training information — 15
Post-sale support information — 14

Note: Up to five responses allowed.
*Industry analyst reports, Gartner Magic Quadrant, influencer evaluations
Source: ITSMA, How B2B Buyers Consume Information Survey, 2016

Figure 6.3 Types of information needed. Up to five responses allowed. *Indicates statistically significant difference. Reproduced from ITSMA How B2B Buyers Consume Information Survey, 2016.

Post sale, the desire for proactive engagement continues; solution providers must follow through on their ideas

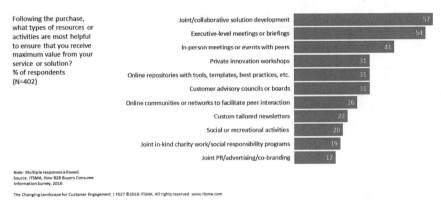

Following the purchase, what types of resources or activities are most helpful to ensure that you receive maximum value from your service or solution?
% of respondents
(N=402)

Joint/collaborative solution development — 57
Executive-level meetings or briefings — 54
In-person meetings or events with peers — 41
Private innovation workshops — 31
Online repositories with tools, templates, best practices, etc. — 31
Customer advisory councils or boards — 31
Online communities or networks to facilitate peer interaction — 26
Custom tailored newsletters — 22
Social or recreational activities — 20
Joint in-kind charity work/social responsibility programs — 19
Joint PR/advertising/co-branding — 17

Note: Multiple responses allowed.
Source: ITSMA, How B2B Buyers Consume Information Survey, 2016

Figure 6.4 Information desired post-sale. Up to five responses allowed. Reproduced from ITSMA How B2B Buyers Consume Information Survey, 2016.

Buyers want engaging and relevant thought leadership not only during the buying process but also after the sale. They seek collaborative solutions, in-person meetings, and customer advisory councils. The buyer's attitude is "OK, we bought your product to solve our business needs. Now, help us make that happen." This is where client engagement is critical. Don't let your company get so carried away with acquiring new names and leads that it neglects thought leadership for current clients.

After the sale, clients want:

- Tools to monitor their return on investment (ROI)
- Templates to monitor usage
- Key Performance Index benchmarks
- Case studies to learn from other companies
- Relevant research

This information should be available to clients in multiple formats, including formats for mobile devices.

Marketers need a regular cadence of pre-sales and post-sales nurturing via insight-led, high-touch programs

Figure 6.5 How marketers can engage clients, from acquiring them to expanding the relationship to retaining them. Up to five responses allowed. Reproduced from ITSMA How B2B Buyers Consume Information Survey, 2016.

Your content must deliver exceptional value

Writing and bringing to market stellar thought leadership is a tough task. So is getting it read. Content is a crowded marketplace. Your piece must stand out with commercial insights. Prospective clients need to see how they can relate these ideas to improving their business.

You're also facing a much savvier customer. Buyers are doing much more research online before phoning suppliers. Indeed, a Corporate Executive Board study of greater than 1,400 B2B customers found that "57 percent of the purchase decision is made before a customer even calls a supplier."[3] This has two important implications: (1) buyers know much more before the initial sales call, and (2) online resources need to be comprehensive.

The Bloom Group explains the imperatives for firms: "It therefore behooves professional services firms to be out there, online, with new ideas and insights when the prospective client is doing that research. That means producing the best thought leadership (with new insights and useful prescriptions), producing it at the right time (when people are looking for a specific kind of help), and getting it in front of those prospective buyers through a variety of channels (on the web, and as printed material and as presentations at conferences and meetings) in a compelling, consistent, and even industrialized way."[4]

Best practices in thought leadership

To consult with outstanding practitioners of thought leadership best practices, the Bloom Group spoke with Russell Craig, FTI Consulting marketing director; Craig Muraskin, Deloitte managing director of innovation; Laura Breslaw, AlixPartners chief marketing officer; and Art Kleiner, editor-in-chief of Booz & Company's management magazine, *strategy+business*.

This interview excerpt is from Tim Parker and David Rosenbaum of the Bloom Group and is provided here courtesy of the Bloom Group.[5] The complete interview is on the Bloomgroup.com site, along with many other compelling blogs worth reading.

Best Practice #1: Align thought leadership with business strategy

If you talk about services you don't provide, who are you helping?

Professional services firms hire smart people who know a lot about a lot and are usually more than happy to share that knowledge. But only some of what they know is relevant to the services their firms offer. Thought leadership that doesn't help a firm sell the services it provides is not useful to the prospective customer, the firm, or the individual practitioners producing it.

> **Thought leadership that doesn't help sell is not useful.**

"We want to make sure that people know that if we put something out there, we can help them with it," says Deloitte's Muraskin. "We're creating thought leadership that's based upon our business expertise, and it has to line up with what we can do for our clients." FTI's Craig says, "We want to showcase our people as leaders in the field, providing innovative, insightful thinking that's expressed in our thought leadership."

If a firm's published thought leadership content is not aligned with its offerings, not only is producing it a waste of time and resources, it risks alienating customers. Customers, says Muraskin, will ask, "Why are they spouting off about something outside their areas of expertise?" A lack of alignment between what a firm offers and what it publishes also risks alienating the firm's internal leadership. "Why are we talking about X? That's not what we do," Muraskin says. "If thought leadership is not relevant to the business," he continues, "the business unit leaders will get tired of it," and the organization's interest in producing it will wane, along with the resources it devotes to it.

However, before thought leadership can be aligned with a firm's business strategy the firm has to have one. You have to ask, Kleiner says, "How much of a distinctive strategy does the firm have? If it doesn't have one, then thought leadership is going to be all over the board and it will largely be driven by individuals pushing an agenda of short-term expedience."

> **Thought leadership marketing sells the value of the firm.**

While thought leadership needs to align with a firm's strategy, it shouldn't be straitjacketed by specific offerings. It's a delicate balance. As Muraskin points out, thought leadership marketing is not the same as sales marketing; thought leadership marketing sells "the value of the firm."

Muraskin allows that some of the material Deloitte publishes is designed not to highlight specific offerings but to "demonstrate our methods and capabilities, our import and influence."

A virtuous cycle for thought leadership production is one in which the thought leadership reinforces the firm's strategy by tracking content development in the firm's various practices. Asking how an article relates to what else the firm is doing "opens up new types of conversations among the thought leaders in the firm," suggests Kleiner, and allows thought leadership "to build on what the firm has already done, thereby deepening the content."

The job of making sure that the thought leadership a firm's subject matter experts are producing aligns with the firm's overall business strategy generally falls to senior leadership on editorial boards and steering committees and to the marketing group.

"The marketing group has overall visibility that can help align content development efforts," FTI's Craig says. "SMEs [subject matter experts] have narrower, practice-centered views," and, adds AlixPartner's Breslaw, tend not to see things "cross-functionally or strategically. That's where marketing comes into play."

But how should marketing organize the means of thought leadership production to create that alignment, while at the same time ensuring that the thought leadership pipeline is properly managed and supplied with the high-quality content that will differentiate the firm and get it noticed?

Best Practice #2: Surround thought leadership development with process

If you don't manage your pipeline, how can you guarantee quality and performance?

Thought leaders at professional services firms are thought leaders because they dive deeply into their subject areas. As Craig said, they focus intensely on what's in front of them. To present thought leadership that aligns with a firm's overall strategy and not just its practices, marketing must play an operational role. Unfortunately, in a business often defined by individuals with (shall we say) large (and, in many cases, well-earned) egos, that's not always easy.

> "Without process, articles can become idiosyncratic, random, and unaligned."

SMEs "don't often think about the audience first," says Breslaw, speaking of her time as director of marketing, Americas, at BCG. "They come to marketing after the fact and ask, 'Help us figure out the audience for distribution purposes.' That is, *after* a piece has been developed. Then it's a scramble to create lists which results in putting execution above strategy." And without support from marketing, all too often, Breslaw says, the SMEs "will have the idea, but rarely follow it through to publication."

To make sure those ideas come to fruition, Breslaw says regular meetings are a must to "ensure that there's a schedule in place so that people are on the same page and the process keeps moving."

"Without process," Craig says, "the tendency will be toward everything being author-driven. The articles may lack supporting research. Without process, articles can become idiosyncratic, suffer from tunnel-vision, and end up random and unaligned."

"We've instituted lots of guidelines on quality," says Muraskin. "We're meticulous about making sure not only that what people are writing about is what they should be writing about, but also that it's the right people writing, people who are approved as leaders within the individual parts of the business. So we have a lot of review to make sure that we're getting the right quality, both in terms of issue selection and how things are written and presented.

"The SMEs are given a lot of support, whether it's professional writers and researchers to work closely with them or their peers. We've created a nice system to make sure that we're giving people the ability to publish and talk and get their voices out there in a way that ensures consistent quality of the deliverable."

For Craig, it's important that the material FTI publishes be presented in a simple, natural manner, avoiding language that is overly academic or stuffy.

Muraskin says, "People were complaining about how now, when they want to write their thought leadership, they have to first write up their business case, abstract it, get it reviewed, and have editors. Some of them were complaining that they could do it all themselves, but they also recognized that the end result was a lot better, and the support was a lot better."

"Not everybody knows how to write, research, and produce," he continues, frankly. "If you want to get writers and researchers to support you and you want the firm's leadership to promote you, and you want marketing to support you, you're not going to get that if you do it on your own."

Process also helps temper the conflicts that inevitably arise between strong-minded individuals convinced that their position is the right one and that the article they've written is perfect. If a process is in place that represents the collective will of the firm, no one person—on an editorial board or in marketing—will be placed in the uncomfortable position of telling an SME that his or her baby is ugly.

Best Practice #3: Make it relevant and timely

If you're not part of the conversation, who will listen to you?

In the news business, timeliness is a given, an obvious necessity. As the Rolling Stones sang, "Who wants yesterday's papers?" The same is true for thought leadership.

A firm's prospective clients are affected by the same events, the same news as everyone else. Within limits, the drivers that move a business to search for a professional services firm are predictable. If, for example, your firm has expertise in the energy space, a major oil spill, or storm, or other newsworthy event that affects that industry is an opportunity to demonstrate your expertise in risk mitigation or alternative energy sources. And an energy company executive looking for the newest thinking on these matters will be more compelled by an article based on, say, the polar vortex of 2014 than by the Great Mississippi Flood of 1927.

To read more of this interview, go to bloomgroup.com/content/best-practitioners-offer-four-best-practices-thought-leadership.

7

Pitfalls in Choosing a Topic

In this chapter:

- Topics to embrace—and topics to avoid
- Why your thought leadership *must express opinions*
- Expert tips on thought leadership best practices

The last chapter covered best practices in content development. Now, let's discuss common pitfalls in selecting topics and how to avoid them. Despite many companies' best efforts, their thought leadership does not always generate significant press or client interest. A major reason why is that firms do not always choose the right issues. They "either probe the same territory covered by other, longer-established studies or fail to address issues more relevant to their prospective audience. Often, the research questions don't enable the firm to display its expertise as they don't reflect its core service offerings."[1]

Criteria for topic selection

The Bloom Group suggests that thought leadership studies should address issues that meet three tests:

- There is **white space** on the topic: issues that haven't been researched before or have been but still lack deep and novel insights.

- The topics are **client hot buttons**: issues on which clients are dying for insights.

- The topics are **company sweet spots**: areas in which the firm has deep expertise and service offerings.[2]

Thought leadership that meets all three criteria is well selected, as illustrated in Figure 7.1 on page 54.

Figure 7.1 Your company's "sweet spot" of expertise meets these three areas. Illustration by Robert Pizzo.

- **Market white spaces** are subjects that the industry wants to know about but that have been little researched. Market white space exists in the gap between your industry's demand for knowledge and the available supply. Your goal is to produce relevant and in-demand content in areas where not much exists.

- **Client hot buttons** are topics that your clients most need to know about. You can identify what your clients are most curious about by studying trade publications, trade conference topics, social media topics, and internet search terms.

- **Company sweet spots** are your firm's areas of expertise and specialization. Consider your subject matter experts and core competencies.

Thought leadership fails when it does not meet all of these criteria, and, unfortunately, some companies' thought leadership doesn't meet any of these criteria.

Bloom Group offers an example that demonstrates the pitfalls of choosing the wrong topic for thought leadership. "Consider a supply chain consulting firm that wants to grow beyond consumer packaged goods and retail. Believing its expertise also applies to industrial goods, the firm decides to survey heavy equipment manufacturers on all their biggest strategic challenges. The firm's aim is to show it understands the sector's most fundamental issues—many of which (perhaps even most) may have little to do with the supply chain. By ignoring or giving little space in the survey to the topic that is its sweet spot—supply chain design and operations—the study is likely to uncover strategic issues that have been covered by others with deeper expertise and experience. What's more, it won't allow the firm to show off the expertise it does have and for which it is known: the supply chain."[3]

> Companies should produce thought leadership on issues readers will hire them to solve.

The point is that the intended audience of industrial equipment manufacturers is probably already familiar with the study's topics. This audience would hire consultants who specialize in the field, not supply chain consultants. The moral is that companies should produce and communicate thought leadership on issues that readers would hire them to solve.

Have opinions—present a point of view

Thought leadership should define a point of view. The value of effective thought leadership is that it presents informed opinions that readers can use in their businesses. Don't weigh down your thought leadership with multiple points of view that say very little. Having different industry players present their opinions can be useful. But a debate that doesn't reach a conclusion or offer a recommendation has little value. At its worst, aimless attempts at thought leadership can yield a seemingly useless series of drafts, sucking up staff resources and money.

The solution is to have a central argument on which there is a consensus. It's recommended that one person have the final decision on the argument and its expression.

Interview with Rob Leavitt, Senior VP at ITSMA

I interviewed Rob Leavitt, senior vice president at ITSMA, a prominent research and advisory company for marketing leaders, about thought leadership best practices.

PK: For companies starting a thought leadership program, what are some of the key steps they need to take? What are the key watch-outs?

RL: The first step, as with any strategic initiative, is to define the business objectives of the program. What are you trying to accomplish? What does success look like? How will this contribute to business growth and innovation?

Next is making sure you have a dedicated leadership team in place. Someone has to own the program, of course, but it's also critical to have cross-functional input and support to guide the effort. This should include senior representatives from marketing, sales, and other parts of the business, such as product or solution development and business leadership. All those groups will contribute to both developing and using your thought leadership with clients, so you want to include them in the planning and governance. The team helps define the most important issues and topics to address and the best ways to promote content, equip salespeople with the ideas, and connect directly with clients and prospects. Thought leadership marketing is a team sport.

A key watch-out is having one-off efforts that produce "random acts of content" not tied to a larger, ongoing strategy and program. Marketers, salespeople, and subject matter experts often want to rush ahead with articles, white papers, or videos on a specific topic or to support a specific campaign without a clear idea of how to support those ideas over time. This typically leads to modest results, at best, and support for the program can fade fast.

PK: In today's exceptionally crowded marketplace, what makes content stand out? How can a company without many resources hope to accomplish this?

RL: The key is carefully picking topics related to a theme that is important to clients and prospects, and producing high-quality content on a regular basis. For smaller companies, this might mean just one or two themes rather than trying to cover a broad range. And you need to bring something new to the table. This could mean finding the "competitive white space," that is, an issue with client interest yet not much written by your competitors. Or, more often, it means providing a different point of view on a familiar topic. "Me-too" material is not thought leadership. But if you can provide new research, a new perspective, or a new approach to addressing a familiar challenge, you have a much better chance of standing out from the crowd.

> "'Me-too' material is not thought leadership. But if you can provide a new perspective or approach, you have a better chance to stand out."

Another big opportunity is working collaboratively with your clients to create new points of view together. Thought leadership programs often take an ivory tower approach, working by themselves on the perfect ideas that they can unveil with great fanfare as the next big thing. But our clients actually know that we don't have all the answers, and they're often happy to participate in the research and development part of thought leadership to figure out new approaches together. Rather than relying just on your internal experts, thought leadership programs should consider organizing executive round-tables, innovation workshops, and other ways to bring in your top clients to explore new approaches together. This can lead to more compelling content and more credible new approaches to bring back into the market. Sometimes the most important task is identifying the right questions to ask.

It's also important that thought leadership have not only a new perspective but a clear voice. No one wants to read or listen to "corporate speak" produced by anonymous experts. You can't have thought leadership without thought leaders! Let your subject matter expert's voice come through. Show off your personality. Elevate the

> "Let your subject matter expert's voice come through. Show off your personality."

visibility of your experts and thought leaders. Provide contact information and make it easy for clients and prospects to connect.

It's also important to stick within the areas that contribute directly to the business. Good thought leadership needs to be educational and nonpromotional, but your clients know it's part of an effort to eventually sell your products and services. Spending a lot of time and energy expounding on issues totally unrelated to your business is usually a waste of time. So the goal should be objective, valuable, educational thought leadership focused on issues that your clients care about, but in areas where your company can help. There needs to be a clear connection between the issues you raise and the solutions you sell.

PK: Which companies are producing noteworthy thought leadership?

RL: The big consulting and professional services firms such as McKinsey, Deloitte, and PwC [PricewaterhouseCoopers] often lead the pack. They've built their business for years on ideas and experts, so they understand the value of creating and marketing thought leadership and invest accordingly. A lot of the big technology firms do a good job, too, such as IBM, Cisco, and Adobe. But a lot of smaller companies are doing a good job in their niches, too.

PK: Should content be gated?

RL: I lean heavily toward providing open content which gets people interested, and then over time asking for personal information as part of a broader effort to build ongoing engagement. You want to make it easy for people to consume your ideas, and you need to provide real value if you're going to ask for a lot of information. Interestingly, ITSMA research shows that business buyers are quite willing to provide personal information if they have confidence that you will use it to provide more personally relevant content. But nothing annoys people more than asking for a lot of information and not providing real value in return.

You also shouldn't ask for information when it's already available from your own systems, such as marketing automation tools, website tracking, and event registrations.

Another issue with gated content to consider is the trend toward "binge content." Think about this as the Netflix of content marketing. When our clients or prospects get interested in a topic, they want to be able to dive in and explore the equivalent of a whole season in short order. So rather than the drip marketing which has been customary—here's a piece, now here's another piece a week later—we should support reader momentum and make it as easy as possible to consume a lot of content in a single sitting. You might gate the fifth or sixth piece, but be careful not to slow the momentum.

PK: Often, thought leadership and content marketing are discussed around B2B companies. Can you discuss effective content marketing for consumer companies?

RL: Good thought leadership has a strong voice and shifts thinking. For consumers, it is accomplished through compelling storytelling. A good example is the Dove ad which challenged the conventional notion of beauty. It brought the topic of diversity into the discussion and, in doing so, changed consumer perception. It was new and different. That's what made it good thought leadership.

PK: What do you think are some of the most important metrics from content marketing/thought leadership programs that senior management should see and judge?

RL: We should think in terms of the three Rs:

Reputation: Are we strengthening our reputation as industry experts and innovators with the clients, prospects, and market influencers who matter most to our business? Do our clients value our content and think of us more as consultants and advisors than just vendors and suppliers?

Relationships: Is our thought leadership marketing effective in cultivating and sustaining relationships with key decision makers at our most important clients and prospects? Are we using our program to build important relationships with business partners and advisors? Is it helping with our internal collaboration across marketing, sales, and other functions?

> "Is our thought leadership marketing effective in cultivating and sustaining relationships with key decision makers at our most important clients and prospects?"

Revenue: Are we seeing new business opportunities triggered by our thought leadership activities? Are salespeople using our ideas and content to have new types of conversations and move faster through the purchase process? Are we more effective in supporting higher value deals and premium pricing based on our industry expertise? Are we improving client satisfaction, loyalty, and interest in innovative new solutions?

8

Editorial Project Planning

In this chapter:

- Creating an editorial plan
- Scheduling content production
- Assembling and managing a creative team

So far, we have discussed content planning, personas, topic selection, and best practices in content development.

Now, it's time to execute. We'll discuss in this section putting together the all-important editorial calendar and look at best ways to produce content.

Scheduling

Once you have decided on topics and personas, the next step is to construct an editorial plan. Come up with a timeline showing which editorial topics and associated pieces will be released and when. Construct a project plan for each piece showing each stakeholder, work that must be completed, and production timelines.

At this point, you should engage with stakeholders to find out how much time they need to complete various stages. You'll want to talk to any graphic arts people, if applicable. You also need to make sure to communicate with your legal or compliance department on what material needs to be reviewed and how long turnarounds will be. If your content will be translated for overseas markets, be sure to understand how much time is needed for translation and incorporate that into your project plan. Other stakeholders can include copywriters, developers, business marketers, and brand managers. It is recommended that you leverage a project management tool to help you. Some of the industry-leading project management tools include Basecamp, Kapost, WorkDay, and Microsoft Project.

Production basics

Another part of your project plan is to identify who will actually produce what content. This may be you and your team, an agency, freelancers, or a combination. There are many substeps to producing content. You need to think through what these are and who will do them.

Key steps in producing content include:

- Interviewing subject matter experts

- Researching topics

- Finding statistics, if applicable

- Searching for visuals or images to employ or creating new ones

- Compiling raw information into a *meaningful story*—fitting research and facts together into an insightful piece

- Laying out and designing the pieces

All these steps may be handled by your team, an agency, or various external players. Your project plan should spell that out. For many companies, a hybrid approach works best. If you use external partners, however, you should have one internal person who is responsible for all the relationships. This individual needs to ensure that all pieces are being produced according to plan, manage the budget and timeline, and troubleshoot. This individual should also communicate clearly your branding and compliance requirements to external partners.

> You should have one person who manages content, the budget, and the timeline.

Note that you can reuse content in multiple formats. So your project plan for your upcoming white paper should address not only its original format but also spin-off formats such as a short report, infographic, or PowerPoint deck. Each should be spelled out in the project plan.

Tip: Try the Content Marketing Institute (contentmarketinginstitute.com) for ideas on content creation and project management.

A kit for coordinating production

You may be trying to coordinate efforts across office locations and countries and from headquarters to subsidiaries. What is the best way to handle this? Pam Didner in *Global Content Marketing* suggests putting together a *content kit* whereby you categorize the content by editorial topics and personas. You would include a description and hyperlink or file share location for each piece. She notes that this is especially important for sharing content plans across local teams.

Didner suggests that a content kit should include:

- An editorial calendar

- A short description of topical story framework and messaging

- Keyword search recommendations

- Top five content recommendations by personas

- A list of detailed content by product or purchase journey[1]

Keep branding in mind when producing content

An essential part of your content kit should be guidance on your brand.

The look and feel of your content across platforms should reflect your brand. Make sure your team and all your agencies have clear brand guidelines. Some branding elements like the logo and company description may already exist. Other decisions may need to be made:

> The look and feel of your content across platforms should reflect your brand.

- What kinds of images do you want to show? Should they fall into a larger theme you are visually trying to convey? For example, do you want to communicate confidence, personableness, or technical know-how?

- Should the company description be altered for content pieces?

- What voice and tone are you striving for? Think this through carefully, because the tone of your content will reflect directly on your company and its brand. Can humor be used? Can any content pieces like blogs be written in first person? Or is an objective narrative voice always needed?

- It's important to maintain your brand across every channel you use, including print, web, mobile, apps, customer portals, and social media. Strive for consistency across disparate channels.

Staff roles

So far we've talked about planning content marketing. Now you are ready to execute. But who will do it? Should you outsource? What kind of budget will you need? In this section, we will discuss the best ways to research, write, edit, and distribute your thought leadership.

It's helpful to think of your staff in the following categories:

- Subject matter experts who will provide the knowledge

- Writing, editing, and graphic arts professionals who will help you present information in an appealing format

- Marketers who will help you bring your content to market

- Public relations professionals who will pitch your content to the media

- Sales professionals who will use your content to persuade clients

- Analysts who will help measure your content's impact

Let's examine the role of these categories and how to manage them effectively.

Subject matter experts

Subject matter experts play a crucial role in providing much of the information and opinion you will use in your content. It's crucial that you put together a network of subject matter experts in your company. They can serve as your advisory committee. A good practice is to formalize the committee with monthly or quarterly meetings. You'll want to select topics and gain commitment from individuals for input. You will interview them for primary research and solicit their opinions on outside individuals to interview and articles to survey. They may also host your webinars, depending on the subject. Some may also write the blogs.

You can also reach outside your firm for subject matter expertise. Your company is not an expert in everything. There are undoubtedly topics you would like to address that no one in your company is really an expert on. This is a good opportunity to ask clients and industry associations to share their expertise. Recognizing the contributions and knowledge of others builds goodwill and adds credibility to your content.

Communications professionals

Let's break this varied category down.

- **Writers:** Some pieces you will probably write yourself or delegate to your team, if you have one. But you can also hire outside writers to manage the workload. Some writers also have areas of expertise that can be helpful. A good writer will attend the research interviews, ask questions, develop the outline, and draft it. This will you get you started, but you still need to play a role in building the outline, researching, writing, and editing.

- **Graphic art director:** This crucial role turns your text into something more visually appealing. The graphic art director designs the page and considers the best layout and the best physical construction of the piece. An excellent graphic arts designer will help you think through a concept and offer suggestions on how to make it work visually.

- **Copy editor:** It's imperative that all your content be error-free. I strongly recommend that you hire a professional copy editor. A good copy editor will check not only for grammar, punctuation, and spelling but also for word choice, consistency, and redundancy. Many copy editors charge a reasonable fee and can turn around work quickly. No matter how many times you look at a piece, you likely won't catch every mistake.

Marketers

Once you have your piece, you will need help bringing it to market. You will want to create emails and landing pages with forms, select email lists of target audiences, post on social media, conduct paid searchers, and employ other channels to maximize your exposure. Depending on your company, this may mean channel owners. You may also choose to outsource some of this work to a website firm or one that specializes in campaign management. Importantly, you must ensure that all the leads captured on your form will be routed effectively. You should conduct testing to verify.

Public relations professionals

If your piece deserves media attention (see chapter 9, "Public Relations"), you will want to consult a public relations professional on pitching it to the right media. You can have a member of your company's internal team manage media relations, but an outside PR firm or freelancer will have expertise and an established network of media contacts. A PR professional will advise you on which parts of your piece are likely of the most interest. He or she can then pitch it to the media in an efficient manner. It is very hard to get a reporter's attention, let alone a commitment to writing a story, so a PR professional can give you essential help.

Sales teams

It's crucial that you communicate your content strategies to sales leaders. You can solicit topics from them. You should also explain to them the value of your content in the sales process. The best practice is to write an email each time you have a new piece. Outline its content and, more importantly, note which products correspond to the content, even if the link is indirect. See chapter 21, "How Thought Leadership Helps Sales," for guidance on setting up an Insights Library.

> It's crucial to communicate your content strategies to sales.

Analysts

After you have produced and published your content, you will want to know how effective it was. If your company has an analytics person, you can collaborate to measure channel performance (email open rate, click-through rate, social media post click rate, etc.), downloads, leads, and any closed sales. More complicated but crucial is working with your analytics person to determine how people who download your piece should be scored for your lead nurturing program.

All these roles are crucial in your putting together a content marketing plan. It's important for your whole team to understand and be committed to your strategy. Make sure to give your team members the big picture of what you are trying to accomplish, as well as assigning them specific tasks. And if you receive accolades on your content pieces, be sure to thank and give credit to all those involved.

Section Two

Engaging the Industry

9

Public Relations

In this chapter:
- Pitching your content to the media
- Content that grabs media attention
- Why information the media wants is not always what your clients need
- Crafting your PR message
- Promoting your content at corporate events

Up till now, we have discussed at length creating a content strategy and executing it. Now, let's discuss how to bring your content to market. In this chapter, we'll talk about what makes your thought leadership valuable to the press. We'll look at the difference between content that interests the media and content that is valuable to your customers. We'll also cover participating in industry events with thought leadership.

Does your content have media interest?
Some of your content will be more valuable to the media, and some will be of greater value to clients. Table 9.1 on page 70 shows the trade-off between PR value and user value. Is it important to have media interest in your content? It depends on your objective. If you are trying to garner a leadership role in your industry, gain influence, and catch the attention of senior executives, then yes. Media coverage of your content also builds brand awareness. But if your objective is to maximize leads, public relations value may be less important. If your target market is

> **Is it important to have media interest in your content? It depends on your objective.**

		Practical Use to Business	
		Low	High
Value to Trade Media	Low	Commonsense articles with clichés that offer no perspective or solutions	How-to guides
	High	In-depth reports or studies	Reports on hot industry topics with unique perspective, proprietary data, and "so whats." May have a bundle of formats: long report, short report, infographic, press release, guide derived from findings, etc.

Table 9.1 Business and trade media value different types of content.

smaller firms, they may prefer more practical content, which is useful but has less media value than statistics-rich reports on industry-wide issues.

What is the media interested in? Generally speaking, reports that are based on proprietary data on timely topics are among the most valuable for the media. Since the data is proprietary, there is no competition. Only your firm can provide that data. If your information is related to an external event that the media is already writing about, reporters will welcome this additional data. For example, consider a company that provides information on the construction industry based on its own research. In a contested presidential election, infrastructure emerges as a hot issue. This firm can then provide a data-based perspective on the election's outcome on infrastructure spending.

> Reports based on proprietary data on timely topics are the most valuable to the media.

Locally based stories are also of value to the media. After all, much of the media covers a metro area or region. Only a few media outlets are national. So if you are an energy consulting firm, your analysis of an oil price drop on local employment in Houston would likely be of interest to Houston-based media. So when you think of content, consider regional or local topics besides national and international ones.

An important best practice is to outline the key issues being discussed for your industry and how your firm can contribute to the conversation. Your public relations professional can coach you on how to do that. Also, the more your subject matter experts speak at conferences, the more likely the media will take notice.

If you work for a business-to-business company, your media targets don't need to be mainstream publications. Trade publications are much more likely to be interested in your content. You should subscribe to and be very familiar with the main newspapers, magazines, and online providers for your industry. Trade publications are often specific to a subindustry, so make sure you know the full range of trades for relevant subindustries. Reading industry magazines may also give you some content ideas.

Trade publications are top media targets for B2B companies.

Knowing these relevant publications is only part of the battle. You will also need to pitch them effectively. This is where an outside specialist can help. Networks and building relationships are very important in this field. After all, reporters juggling many stories and deadlines need to know they can trust you.

If you work for a consumer company, you'll need to think of a unique angle to attract the reporter's attention. This can be a unique community event, something seasonal, or participation in a sponsorship or contest that has value to a publication's readership.

Tips for making your content more attractive to the media

Here are some tips for both consumer and business-to-business companies to make public relations and media outreach more enticing to reporters:

- Try embargoing content to provide your most important findings to a select group of reporters before its scheduled publication. This allows reporters time to familiarize themselves with your content so they can write an article in due time.

- Consider offering exclusives on your proprietary content to a select group of reporters. Reporters are more likely to feel invested in your story if they know few others will be covering it. That exclusivity makes their coverage of it rare and more valuable to the reader and their publication. However, this works only with highly anticipated and primary content that no other company would produce. There is a trade-off here, though.

Exclusivity necessarily means losing breadth of coverage. Weigh the risk and the rewards.

- For your proprietary reports, try a tiered pitching strategy. First, pitch it to various business media outlets. Then, try the trades. Attempt to find one who won't just mention your report but will run a piece on it. When you do find it, you can repurpose your pitch into a byline article that the reporter may be interested in.

- Understand each publication's readership. If a publication refuses to cover a particular topic, try to figure out which topics will interest its readers. Maybe your report is too esoteric. Can you repurpose it so that it connects with a typical professional in your industry? For example, if your report is on risk management, can you make it compelling to the typical insurance agent on Main Street?

- For local business media, try offering top ten lists. For example, if you are pitching the Rochester, New York–based *Rochester Business Journal* on a merger/acquisition report your company has put out, frame it as "Top 10 Acquisitions This Year in Rochester, NY, Metro Area." Find the most appealing hook for each reporter.

- Another tip for local business media: try pitching a year-in-review article about a metro area. It's a chance to present local data, interpret it, and show how it does or does not fit into a larger trend. January or February is usually the right time to review the past year.

Crafting your PR message

Your PR message should also align with your brand strategy. To put this into practice, ask yourself the following questions:

- How is your corporate identity viewed by the media and the public? How do you want to change that, if at all?

- What is the boilerplate messaging about your company? Is this represented on your press releases? Or does the message need to be tailored?

- What is your company's elevator pitch? Does the media respond to it? Or does your pitch need to be modified? Seek feedback from reporters you trust and your publicist or public relations firm.

- Are you delivering your PR messaging through your social media channels effectively? To answer this, you will need to analyze your social channels' press release posts for engagement. Look at likes, shares, comments, tweets, clicks, and how many people download your content or view your website's Newsroom page. Google Analytics can also give you some of this information on an aggregated level. Google Analytics won't give you personally identifiable information because of Google's privacy rules, but it will give you overall page traffic information.

- Have you identified the key influencers in your industry? Make sure that they are following you on social media. You should be following them, retweeting them, and engaging with their posts. You can sometimes reach out to industry influencers with exclusive or embargoed content. It's essential that key influencers know what you are producing and that they see value in it for their channels' audiences.

Your website should have an easily navigable Newsroom section. Most Newsroom pages list press releases from the company in chronological order. You should also have an About Us section that lists the articles that have been written about your company. An About Us section is in some ways more important than a Newsroom page. Any company can put out press releases, and press releases are often seen as merely self-serving. But articles written by noted publications give your company cachet and show that your products, content, and executives are worthy of media attention.

> **Press releases are often seen as self-serving—but articles by noted publications give your company cachet.**

Presenting your content through events

Attending or hosting corporate events is an opportunity to present your content to both the industry and the media. There are three primary ways you can promote your content at these events:

- **At your company's booth:** Print out your white papers, reports, infographics, surveys, and other items that you think will be most relevant to attendees. Consider the best printing options to present each piece. Long content might be printed as a bound book or report, while short-form content might be repackaged as a foldout option, such as a brochure. You might also try creating a postcard with a link (or perhaps an easy-to-remember URL alias) to your website's content.

You may also want to display some of your content on screens at your booth. As conference attendees come to your booth, your company's representatives can offer them relevant content. It's important not to overwhelm attendees with irrelevant information. Ask attendees about their needs, business problems, and questions, and offer them the content that will help them the most. Also offer them subscriptions to your e-newsletters and sign-ups on your social media channels.

- **Speaking events:** Try to book your subject matter experts at the conference's panels and lectures. This is a very effective way to raise awareness of your company's thought leaders among your industry's top people. The best way to get your thought leaders speaking opportunities is to obtain a copy of the conference's agenda early and speak to organizers about which panels your experts can contribute to and what information and insights they can offer. You can also propose one of your thought leaders as a panel moderator. Your subject matter expert can construct the panel's theme, introduce participants, ask questions and follow-up questions, keep panelists' answers on track, summarize key points, and route audience questions.

You may also want to videotape your subject matter experts at the conference. Ask them questions related to the conference's theme. You can overlay excerpts from these interviews with segments from speakers. This would make a great video for your company's YouTube page and website.

- **Social media:** Live tweeting from your event is essential. If it's your company's own conference, make sure to create an engaging yet succinct hashtag. Announce this tag and feature it on your content literature. Put out interesting quotes, insights, and statistics discussed at the conference. Make sure your tweets include a call to action where users can see more. Depending on the specific tweet, you will want to drive users to a content piece or a conference page. Don't make these too self-promotional. You can also post to your other channels such as Facebook, Instagram, YouTube, and others. As is always the case with social media, listening is as important as posting. So respond to others' posts. Thank them for retweeting and you should retweet others as appropriate. Answer questions when posed. Build on conversations.

10

Creating a Section on Your Website for Thought Leadership

In this chapter:

- Presenting content on your website
- Spotlighting your best thought leadership
- Functional web elements for content pages
- Designing for mobile
- Sharing content with other websites

Now that you are creating noteworthy content, you need to have a home for it. You will need a page that aggregates all of your content on your website. This will make your content more searchable and improve your Google ranking. But putting your content in one place also showcases your thought leadership as a whole, transforming it from a series of one-off promotions to a holistic perspective on your industry—which is real thought leadership.

Your thought leadership page can be named "Resource Center" or "Insights" or something similar. The best way to set up the page is by theme. For the user, the topic is more important than format. So when you look at all your content, determine what themes emerge from your material. Try to identify at least four themes. Map all your content against them. This becomes the framework for the page. Describe each theme with clear "so whats" for the reader. See Figure 10.1 on page 76 for an example.

This example from Broadridge Financial Solutions, an investor communications and financial technology company, shows the thought leadership grouped by theme. Experts are also listed along with their LinkedIn profiles.

Each piece that falls under the themes needs an image and a two- to three-sentence description. The pieces should be gated so that when users download them, they will need to enter their information. The forms should have only

Figure 10.1 Example of a thought leadership resource page.

about five to seven fields, such as name, company name, email address, and phone number. You can also include fields to determine whether the user is right for your business. For example, if you only service companies with more than 1,000 employees, you can include a question on employee count along with a pull-down menu. But keep the number of fields to a minimum. Otherwise, you may lose users and drive up bounce rates. There should also be a checkbox in case users would like your company to contact them right away. Your content pieces can be in PDF or HTML format. The latter may carry additional search-within-document functionality and possibly yield more SEO benefits.

Functional elements

What about subsequent user visits? Will users have to fill out the same form on your website every time they visit? As we will see in chapter 12, "Building a Campaign Landing Page," you should use progressive profiling, in which you ask the user different questions in each visit. So in the second visit, you can ask the user questions about the company's industry or revenue range. But don't ask questions that you can just research or use a list matching service to find out. As a rule of thumb, after the fourth visit, the visitor should no longer have to fill out forms to see content.

Here are other functional elements to pay attention to in building your Insights page:

- Include clearly marked icons for sharing each content piece. The standard set of sharing icons includes email, LinkedIn, Twitter, Facebook, and the ability to print. If you are presenting a highly visual medium that is more consumer-oriented, include Instagram and Pinterest. You don't need to include all social media icons. Display only those most relevant to your audience.

- You can have an intermediate page between the Insights home page and the actual content (PDF or HTML). This page's job is to entice the user to download the piece. It should include a concise yet compelling description of the content piece's main idea and a graphic of the content piece, plus other visual elements like banners to make the page appealing. Last, this intermediate page should include a contact form for the user to fill out and a link to download the piece.

- Add a Subscribe button to the Insights home page. This is very important, because if you can add subscribers, you can push out content to a targeted audience rather than always having to pull them in through various promotions. Subscriptions can be to e-newsletters. These newsletters can be a summary of your content pieces by theme, such as "Five Most Popular," "Classics," or "Highlights."

- Another very user-friendly feature is to place relevant articles in the right-hand side margin or lower pane. This is like the classic Amazon "Frequently Bought Together" or "Customer Who Bought This Item Also Bought" tactic. You'll need to map each content piece to relevant pieces. Displaying these suggestions in context is an unobtrusive way to further engage users.

- Search on your Insights page is critical. It can make or break the user experience. The topic is the most important feature to search by. So include a drop-down button on the top of the page listing all your key topics. Next to that can be a drop-down by content format (article, webinar, white paper, guide, etc.).

- Consider also placing a photo of the subject matter experts in your company and their LinkedIn profiles and email addresses next to their contributions. Link to your Executive Profiles section, if your website has one. This is a seamless way to introduce your company's experts and to increase their networks. It's also an indirect way of generating more sales.

Designing for mobile

Everyone knows that all web pages have to be mobile adaptive. So your Insights page must reconfigure for both smartphones and tablets. You should test this extensively to ensure proper functionality. But making your page mobile friendly is more than pure page adaptability. You may want to call out content pieces that are particularly well suited for mobile. You can even categorize them as "Mobile Insights."

One possibility for mobile content is podcasts. You can have conversations with experts on pertinent topics that matter to your prospects and clients. This is yet another chance to showcase your company's experts. An interview can be more exploratory than didactic. In other words, while webinars, guides, and reports have a defined set of information to convey, this is more to discuss ideas and generate perspectives. The podcast interviewer's follow-up questions and conclusions depend on the interviewee's responses. That makes it more interesting to the listener.

Your podcasts should offer a transcript for those who want to read it. A transcript may also provide additional SEO benefit. The ability to play the podcast would be on all channels. What makes it mobile friendly, though, is that users can subscribe to your podcast. The current dominant media for aggregating mobile podcasts for your subscribers are Google Play and Apple iTunes.

Highlighting your best content

Consider creating a Featured Insights section for your best content pieces. These are content pieces you have reason to believe will be the most popular, or they may be groundbreaking in some way. You probably don't want to pick pieces that are too narrow or focused on niche topics. You can also analyze which pieces receive the most page views and downloads and make those your featured content. Usually, this section would appear toward the top of the page.

To comment, or not to comment?

Should you allow comments on your content? There are pros and cons to that. On the positive side, you are encouraging users to interact and create a discussion. It creates a two-way conversation. On the con side, comments sections often do not work well. Most business-to-business users do not leave comments. Some are from highly regulated industries so they may be afraid to leave comments. In the consumer space, many comments are inappropriate or inane. If you choose to enable comments, you will definitely need to monitor them.

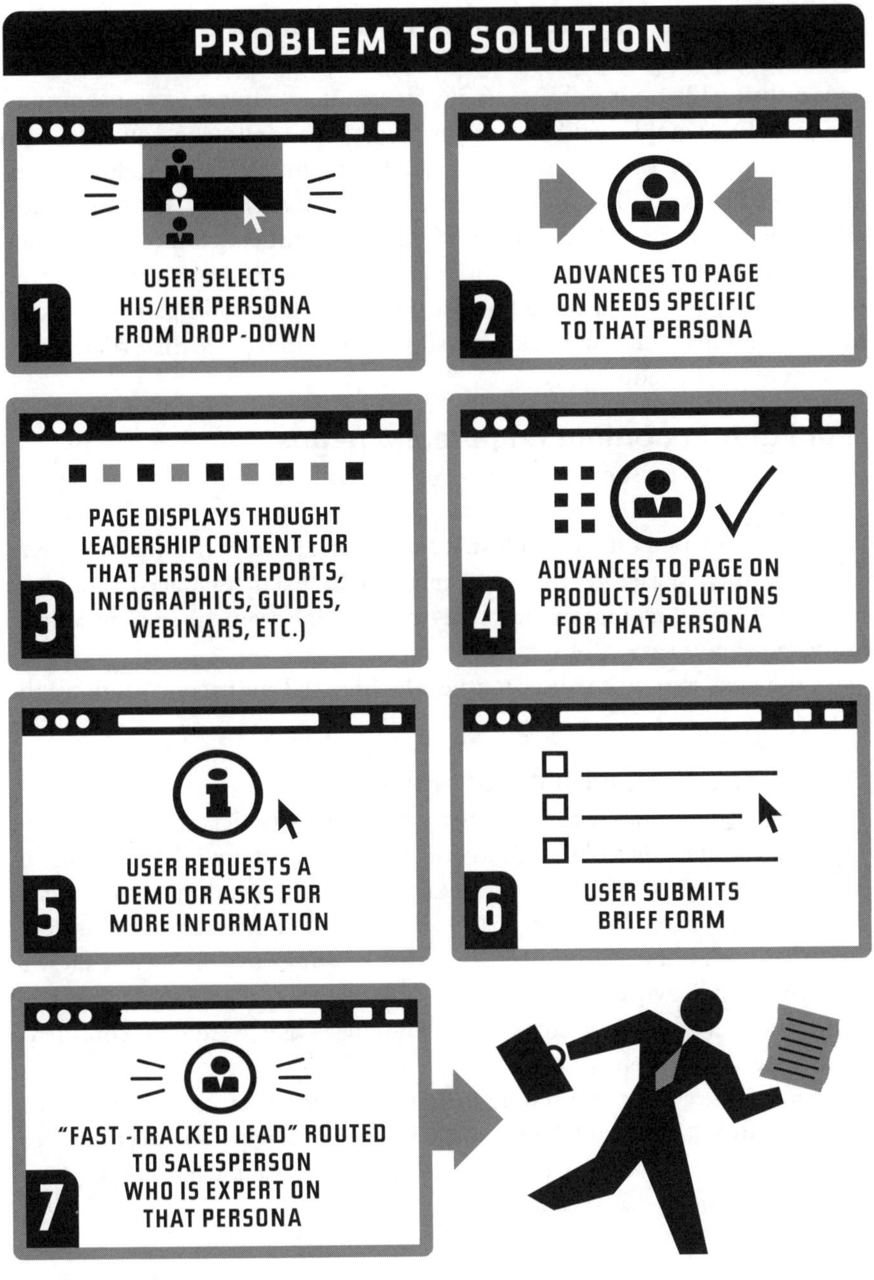

PROBLEM TO SOLUTION

1 USER SELECTS HIS/HER PERSONA FROM DROP-DOWN

2 ADVANCES TO PAGE ON NEEDS SPECIFIC TO THAT PERSONA

3 PAGE DISPLAYS THOUGHT LEADERSHIP CONTENT FOR THAT PERSON (REPORTS, INFOGRAPHICS, GUIDES, WEBINARS, ETC.)

4 ADVANCES TO PAGE ON PRODUCTS/SOLUTIONS FOR THAT PERSONA

5 USER REQUESTS A DEMO OR ASKS FOR MORE INFORMATION

6 USER SUBMITS BRIEF FORM

7 "FAST-TRACKED LEAD" ROUTED TO SALESPERSON WHO IS EXPERT ON THAT PERSONA

Figure 10.2 A persona page can bring a client directly from their particular problem to a solution—and a sale. Illustration by Robert Pizzo.

Other ways to highlight content on your website

Besides the Insights page, there are other important places for content on your website. On your website, see if you can place a frame of your Featured Insights. This would then link to your Insights page and consequently drive more traffic. You can also include related content on your product pages. This can be content directly related to the product, such as a client case study referencing a product. But content with a more indirect connection to your product can also be compelling. For example, you may have an article on how your industry is more focused on cost tracking. This would pair well with a solution you may offer on tracking cost, so you should place this article at the bottom of your product page.

Highlighting content on persona pages

If your site has persona pages, place relevant content on them. Persona pages speak to a particular business type (see chapter 4, "Defining Your Audience"). Personas vary based on your industry. It's essentially your customer segment. The page then speaks to that segment's needs. Each user need should be mapped to a product that answers that need. Placing segment-specific content on these pages is very effective.

It's the next step on the user journey. Figure 10.2 on page 79 outlines the key steps.

Sharing content with other websites

You can also partner with webmasters of third-party sites to share content. Your site can include links to third-party sites that offer additional insights. As part of the partnership arrangement, that website would include links to your Insights page. If the third-party site is highly trafficked, Google interprets that site as having authority, so if that site links to yours, your site will gain "street cred" with Google and will rank higher. It's like in middle school when students who hung out with the "popular" kids were then considered more popular themselves.

On a technical note, you should definitely employ a screener to ensure that bots don't invade your site. Your site's developer can help you select the most appropriate one and add it to your site. Typically, users will type displayed characters to prove that they are not a bot.

11

Blogging

In this chapter:

- Using blogs to promote your company as a thought leader
- Expanding and engaging your audience
- Integrating blogging into your content plan
- Managing blog editorial projects
- Working with guest bloggers
- SEO for blogs
- Measuring blogging success

An integral part of your content marketing should be developing blogs. They are a cost-effective way of engaging your audience in bite-size chunks.

Why should you spend resources on blogging? How will a blog help your business move forward? These are common questions. While the specifics vary by industry and company, here are some overall justifications:

- A well-done blog can help change the perception of your firm. If your company has been thought of as just another vendor, blogs and other content will help your company be seen more as a thought leader.

- While websites and marketing materials are passive, a blog with updates and interactivity from users creates a dynamic relationship inviting users to come back.

- When the right keywords are employed, blogs can improve search engine optimization.

- Blogs increase the number of web pages on your site, as each blog article is a separate page, giving more chances for your sites to show up in higher rankings from keyword searches on Google, Bing, and Yahoo.

- If you have excellent or unique content, other websites are likely to link to it. These inbound links increase user traffic, and search engines calculate these as authoritative hubs.

Blogs often work best when they have a theme and are updated frequently. Publishing a new blog post once a week is probably ideal, but if that is too demanding, try for at least once per month. If you can blog only monthly, let your readers know your schedule to set their expectations.

To set up a blog, you can take advantage of preexisting platforms. The most popular and one of the easiest to use is WordPress.com. Importantly, you must host the blog on your company's own domain, not that of the external provider. The reason is that you want your company's site to capture the domain authority from inbound links. So have your blog address be your-company.com/blog or as a subdomain at blog.yourcompany.com.

It's important to host your blog on your own domain.

Here are some essential elements for your blog:

- Social media share icons

- A comments section—but monitor comments and respond or delete when necessary

- Options to subscribe to your email or e-newsletter to alert subscribers to new blog posts

Blog topics

Your aim is to select those industry-relevant issues that readers care about or are struggling with. To start out, it is preferable for blogs to be restricted to just a few themes to gain credibility with readers and within the industry. You want to guard against spreading yourself too thin by having a completely different topic each week. Your blog gives you a chance to be known for something, to advance a perspective, or to put forth facts and insights that help the reader.

Go back to the content plan that we discussed earlier in chapter 2. When you reference your content plan, see which topics resonate with your audience and also where your company has expertise. Use this as the raw material from which to create your blogging ideas.

Editorial calendar

You should create a blogging calendar with these elements:

- Date
- Topic
- One sentence takeaway
- Image or video to include
- Who will write the blog
- Keywords or tags

Glancing at your editorial calendar across a few months will help you see how topics are related to each other. You can create umbrella themes for your blog topics. This will be important in your marketing copy and social media posts discussing your blogs and why a user should read them.

Guest bloggers

Besides creating original blogs, you can enlist guest bloggers. These can be industry insiders, clients, analysts, and other bloggers. Guest bloggers are an excellent complement to your original blogs for these reasons:

- Guest bloggers increase exposure of your blogs to the industry.
- Blogs from well-known industry players can be media-worthy events that your public relations team can leverage.
- Exposure through the guest blogger's network will be much larger. This will be amplified on social media through sharing.
- Guest bloggers increase web traffic to your site and potentially more inbound links from other blogs and industry websites. This will greatly aid your site's search engine optimization.
- Logistically, using guest bloggers lightens your workload in having to constantly create new posts.

From your guest blogger's standpoint, there are also benefits:

- Exposure to a new audience.
- Increased domain authority through linking from your site to your guest blogger's site.
- Creative stimulus of writing for a new audience.

Who will write them?

There should be one point of contact for blogging at your company. This can be someone in public relations or in marketing. Without one person taking ownership, there is a fairly high risk that the project will live for a while and then fall through the cracks once people get busier.

But the owner of the blogs does not have to write all of them. Part of the mission is to identify those subject matter experts in the company and sell them on the benefits of blogging. This may be difficult for a few reasons. They may not be used to thinking of themselves as subject matter experts. Also, they may not see the value in it. Some may be concerned about advancing an opinion in a public space.

Though the blog owner does not have to write all the blogs, he or she may have to do some of the work for the internal company bloggers. The blog owner can write questions for subject matter experts to answer or can interview them through text or video. In some cases, the blog owner may have to ghostwrite a draft of the blog for the internal subject matter expert to approve.

Writing, of course, is just one of the phases. Even after the internal subject matter expert develops a draft, the blog owner must edit it and ensure that any direct quotation is sourced and that any images or videos are licensed. Your subject matter expert is probably unfamiliar with SEO practices. Thus, the blog owner will need to create keyword tags and SEO-friendly headlines, metadata, and alt text for photos.

SEO for blogs

Key elements for robust SEO to include in your blog:

- **Title:** The search engines will try to match the titles to the keywords searched. So consider using phrases in your titles that users are likely to search by. The title of course should also summarize your blog and be catchy. But if the title is too abstract, the blog may be penalized in search engine rankings.

- **Anchor texts:** Within the blog, search key phrases and make them hyperlinks. The user would be able to click on them and arrive at another page on your site, another one of your company's websites, or an external article, blog, report, or website.

- **Links between posts:** One advantage of having blogs under an umbrella theme is that you can link between them. This increases web traffic, SEO, and the user experience. By creating hyperlinked words between blogs, you help the reader see the bigger picture.

Blog titles

To create catchy titles, consider the following:

- A numbered list, like "10 Best Ways to Hire a Contractor."

- Famous individuals' perspectives, like "What You Can Learn from Steve Jobs's Approach to Product Design."

- A question that titillates the reader, like "Are You Getting Outsmarted in Bids?"

- A strong perspective that the reader will be curious about, like "Best Practices in Writing PowerPoint Slides."

Promoting blogs

Try several channels for promoting your blog to potential readers. Through tagging the URL of your post, you will be able to see in Google Analytics which source produced the most traffic to your posting. Social media channels are imperative for promotion. Write a post customized for LinkedIn, Twitter, and Facebook. The unique posting for each channel should reflect the language, audience, and character limits for each. All social media posts should have an image. Perhaps the most important part of posting on social media sites is encouraging users to share your content with their followers. It is through this social media amplification that you will expand your reach exponentially.

Social bookmarking sites are also important for finding more readers. Ask that your readers leverage their social bookmarking sites to increase exposure. On sites such as Reddit, users will often vote on favorite articles. So if your topic resonates, you stand a good chance of receiving far more exposure. The challenge, though, is that your topics may be specialized, technical, or industry-specific. This will make it less relevant to a general bookmarking site audience. To combat this, find a compelling angle for your blog in which many readers would likely be interested.

Finding your blog's audience

There is an old adage: "Fish where the fish are." The same is true for finding your blogging audience. Research what sites those in your industry visit. Which blogs do they read? You should engage in these sites through commenting, linking, and sharing their associated posts in your own social media.

To efficiently aggregate blogs on your topic, use an RSS reader. This will do the work of visiting the various sites and finding the latest blogs, a time-consuming process. There is a plethora of readers to choose from. Be careful of some, though. They may require downloading, which can sometimes lead to viruses. Feedly.com is highly recommended. The service will alert you to new articles. You should also subscribe to various industry blogs. If there are many, prioritize them by relevance to your company and the likelihood of your prospects and clients visiting them. Utilize a service like Website.grader. com to ascertain their domain authority.

There may also be key forums where you can not only post but inspire discussions around your blog. The best-known example is LinkedIn groups. Find lively, interactive groups for your industry where real discussions are taking place. Avoid those that are primarily vendors trying to sell something or job seekers.

Increasing engagement

Another important promotional tactic is including links in your e-news-letter and emailing it to a select group of clients who you think may be interested. Ask recipients to share your posts and to subscribe. But be selective and email only your best blogs.

Also ask for users to comment. If you don't ask, they are unlikely to do so. You can use language like "Please share your thoughts below." You can set up the system so you are emailed every time a user makes a comment. This is very important, because you won't have to constantly monitor your blog for comments. When one is posted, you can respond or not. There are pros and cons to leaving a particularly negative comment up. By not deleting it, you are showing an authenticity that users will appreciate. However, you should develop standards. If the user writes offensive or profane language, you should delete those comments right away.

Measuring your blogging success

Set up a dashboard with metrics to determine engagement levels. Here are key metrics to consider:

- Number of visitors to your blog

- Number of qualified leads that come to you from your blog

- Report on the above two by blog topic

- Number of inbound links from other sites

Section Three

Channels, Campaign Automation, and Tracking

12

Building a Campaign Landing Page

In this chapter:

- Why you should send users to a dedicated landing page—*not* your home page
- Gated vs. ungated content
- Minimizing user annoyances and maximizing user conversions
- Developing long-term relationships with users
- Protecting user privacy
- Measuring conversion rates

So now you have your section on your website for thought leadership. But where will you drive users when they click on links to various content? The short answer is a landing page that you create for the campaign.

Many marketers plan to send campaign responders to their website home page or section on thought leadership. This is faulty for several reasons. Home pages tend to be cluttered with information—descriptions about the company, its history, a career section, awards won (which most users have never heard of), and a variety of products. Most of this information is irrelevant and overwhelming for the prospect. If users click on a link that is supposed to deliver a piece of content, they do not want to waste time searching for it. Home pages often get in the way of users finding your content.

So you are faced with a decision. You can bring users to a cleaned-up home page that has a clear demarcation for the content in question. This could be what's referred to as the "hero" of the page, meaning the eye-catching central image at the top of the page, or it can be a sidebar text and image. The advantage to bringing users to a modified home page is that they may learn more about the company and stay on your website. But the disadvantages of this approach usually outweigh the advantages. Users may feel frustrated in not seeing the content they clicked for and leave the page. Worse, users may feel that you cheated them with a bait and switch. You promised them useful content, but you dumped them on your company's home page.

As noted above, the better option is to create a landing page specifically for that campaign. Building a landing page is an art within itself. It will require testing to see which approach is most effective for your users.

Gating content

You also need to decide whether you are going to "gate" your content. Gating means requiring users to fill out a form giving their personal contact information in order to access the content. Companies vary on this decision. Some insist that only through gaining contact info can they justify the costs and effort of doing thought leadership. However, several experts in thought leadership caution against gating. Tim Parker, partner at the Bloom Group, weighed in on this issue in my interview with him.

"Our philosophy is to almost never gate content. Thought leadership marketing is of course inbound, or pull, marketing, so it makes more sense to me to publish it and let people come to it. There might be conditions under which you put up a gate, but it needs to be clear that the material is good—you have to tell people enough specifics so they can judge if it will be useful to them. 'Our Thoughts on Cybersecurity' doesn't count. 'Our Survey of 500 CIOs That Shows Which Cybersecurity Measures Work' would. Otherwise, most people won't fill the form because of the trouble, and because they don't want to be bothered with follow-up calls."

> "Thought leadership is inbound, or pull, marketing, so it makes sense to publish and let people come to it."

Parker noted though that thought leadership marketing need not be passive. "We have clients who use TL as the content for targeted marketing—specific roles in specific firms—and they too have great success. TL should be actively marketed, but gating it will make it less effective."

If you're going to gate, do it right

If you have reasons for gating your content, here are some tips on gating effectively:

- Your marketing automation tool may be able to build the landing page, which will save you significant costs compared to paying for additional software or using the services of an agency.

- Keep the content simple. Don't overwhelm the user. Make the content piece the hero.

- Use attractive visuals in keeping with your brand. If possible, use images that also convey the message of the content. If you can't find any, use images that promote your brand. Try to avoid cliché or overused images. Always ensure that any image used is licensed with your company to avoid any copyright issues. You might also search for rights-free images.

- Use only one call to action. That should be to download content or whatever your campaign goal is. Be explicit in the value proposition. Users should know exactly what they're getting by investing time in looking at the landing page and in downloading the content. How do you make the user benefit clear? Use specific and descriptive titles, such as "50-point checklist on what to look for in a vendor" or "10 slides on latest trends in industry X" or "ROI calculator."

- Showcase your firm's credibility, particularly if your company is little known. In the consumer space, the Better Business Bureau seal carries weight. Any certifications or industry-recognized awards can also add to the credibility, but don't put up little-known awards that will not add any clout. Client testimonials may help too, but be careful—you don't want the page to be cluttered or bragging. Use endorsements sparingly. Everything you add should meet these criteria: (1) "Will this increase the user's confidence in my company?"; (2) "Will the user trust that my company is legitimate?"; or (3) "Will the user feel more comfortable entering personal information in the form as a result?"

- Make sure to use language addressing users' needs rather than merely describing the content. For example, don't just outline what is in a report, but explain why the user should care. A headline like "Insights into shareholder voting patterns" is vague and irrelevant to users' concerns. You can create more interest by highlighting "Learn what is important to shareholders to create better investor communications."

> Use language addressing users' needs rather than merely describing the content.

What you *must* include on your landing page

Here are elements you should always include on landing pages:

- Always include the company's contact information, including the phone number and email address.

- If you want to encourage sharing of your content, include social media icons for users to easily share links on their Facebook, LinkedIn, or Twitter accounts.

- Make sure all information is on the initial screen without the user having to scroll down to view it. The user may never scroll down and miss that key information.

- Use a layout that is scannable. Remember, users rarely read web pages in a linear fashion. They scan around the page for headlines that grab their attention and read what is underneath. Users are often guided more by images than words. Brief paragraphs, bolded subheadings, bulleted lists, and images are critical.

- It is crucial that you write landing page text designed for SEO (search engine optimization) and SEM (search engine marketing). The easiest way to do this is to include commonly used keywords that a user is likely to search on. Your headlines and subheads should also feature common keywords.

Maximizing conversion rates

Here are three points to consider to help you maximize conversion rates:

- Email users the content, rather than redirecting them to the content piece on another page. This way, the user is forced to give an authentic email. You can also insist on a work email address. To make sure users give their work email, label the field "work email address" and do not allow common domains such as Gmail, AOL, Yahoo, or Hotmail. Marketing automation tools or form hosting providers can verify email domains in seconds and display an error message to the user if validation rules are broken. You can use language like "Please fill out the form to have the report emailed to you." This should increase the likelihood of valid business email addresses.

- Don't make users fill out more than five or six fields. Unless they are highly engaged, users will get tired of filling out the information and leave the landing page. Some data is essential, such as name, company name, and email address, but make it a goal to not ask users to answer the same question twice on different visits. Content management systems and automated marketing tools offer smart profiling features, which ask the user to fill out different fields on each visit, allowing you to gradually build a more complete profile of each user.

- Employ time-savers like drop-down menus and checkboxes. Don't let users create their own answers; require them to select from a list of standardized responses. Tabulating responses at an aggregate level for analysis will be difficult later on if all the responses are unique. By using a drop-down menu or forcing users to choose certain phrases, you will ensure response consistency for all users and make future analyses far easier.

An example of smart profiling

Here is an example of how smart profiling gradually creates a profile of a user:

- **First visit:** User is asked for his or her first name, last name, company name, title, company address, and company email address.

- **Second visit:** User is asked for the number of employees at his or her company, the company's annual revenue, and the number of years user has been at the company.

- **Third visit:** User is asked to select from a drop-down menu which services he or she is primarily interested in.

Note that smart profiling must be used on all pages across your site. If the user revisits the site on a different page for another campaign and wants to download content again, the questions should advance to the next tier, even though it is a different campaign.

When to *not* gate content

Paradoxically, in some cases you may want to give away content without asking for the user's information. There are reasons to do this even if lead generation is a major campaign goal. Some content is PR-worthy—that is, it has proprietary data, discusses a timely topic, or has a unique perspective. This type of content is a good candidate for trade presses such as magazines, blogs, newspapers, or even a TV or radio spot on a business show. In that case, you may want to maximize views of the content.

Giving away content doesn't necessarily mean losing a conversion opportunity. Even if you don't obtain self-generated user information, you will still identify users with a cookie and retarget them. (For more on retargeting, see chapter 16, "Pay-Per-Click Advertising.") It's ultimately a trade-off of high-quality user information versus promotion of your content and brand. Such a decision is best discussed with the public relations and business marketing professionals at your company or client.

But sometimes giving away content can actually increase conversions. Some companies, for example, have not required users to sign up for webinars. When users view the webinar, there is an optional form to fill out for more information. Some companies report that about 20 percent of attendees have filled out the form to obtain more information during the webinar, even though doing so was not required.

Your call to action must appeal to users' self-interest

In prioritizing your time and resources for your landing page, at the top of your to-do list should be creating a compelling call to action. This is one of the most significant variables in yielding higher conversion rates.

Put yourself in the users' shoes. They saw a piece of your content, perhaps on your email or LinkedIn posting, and were intrigued. Then they took a leap of faith and clicked on your link to arrive on your landing page. From the users' perspective, now you have shifted the game. You are asking something of the users—usually their contact information—in exchange for the content. As a result, users who started out curious and open to your content are now questioning whether this transaction is worth it. Their contact information serves as the currency in the transaction. Users will weigh whether giving out their contact information is worth the value of the content.

> Users must feel that your content will help them in their job.

If you can reduce pain points in this process, users will decide it is a worthwhile exchange. At the top of the users' concerns is their privacy. Because spam and telemarketing calls are annoying many users these days, your statement on what you will do with their data is of paramount importance. Make clear that you will not sell or rent their names to any third party.

Next you want to make the process as simple as possible. This is where a short call to action and asking only a few questions of the user come into play.

Then, you need to answer why the user should bother with this transaction at all. The answer lies in the benefit of the content. Users must feel that it will help them in their job, be better informed for an upcoming meeting or presentation, "look smart," or have more knowledge and skills to make them more valuable to future employers.

In a sense, users want it both ways. They want a lot of value from content, yet they often don't want to spend much time and energy consuming it. So by teasing out key insights, facts, statistics, and "must-know" industry trends, you will entice them further. The offer of free content is one tactic we have discussed. Another is expert consultation, which can work well in that the user gets particular questions answered and, hopefully, helpful guidance. Your company gets to establish or further the client relationship and understand the client's needs and tailor answers accordingly.

Make your call to action stand out

No matter what the offer, your call to action needs to stand out. Consider implementing the following:

- Have the call to action stand out visually. Try different colors and font sizes (but nothing too large). Think of it as a clickable image rather just text. Stand back from your landing page and glance at it. In one look, do you notice the call to action, or do you have to hunt around for it?

- The action should communicate the benefit to the user. For example, "Download the white paper" is not compelling, sounds like a lot of work, and has no urgency. The user will ask, "Why should I?" Instead, try something like "View Best & Worst Practices" or "See How Your Company Stacks Up" for a benchmark report.

You may want to rethink your site's journey. In the past, the point of user entry was almost always through the home page. But that is changing. Search engine criteria rank web pages, not websites. Search engines are seeking relevance of a web page to keywords searched. Therefore, every page of your website can be a port of entry for the user and should be treated as such. Every page should have a way of optimizing prospect conversion opportunities. Provide users with multiple opportunities to respond to your site's calls to action.

Designing the landing page

Marketing automation tools will support the creation of campaign-tailored dedicated landing pages without requiring laborious coding. The WYSIWYG

(What You See Is What You Get) graphical interface enables the user to "drag and drop elements into the header, content or footer sections of your landing pages and to easily format your page using HTML, rich text, built-in image hosting, and other formatting options to match the look and feel of your brand."[1]

As you design your landing page, you need to ask these questions:

- Does the page optimize conversions?
- Is the page's text going to yield the best search results?
- Are there enough separate audience segments viewing the landing page to justify creating different versions for each?
- Is the contact information easy?
- Does the user form visibly stand out?
- Is the process for the user cumbersome? What are potential pain points for the user, such as being asked for too much information or having to search to find key information?

Developing a long-term relationship with users

Many think of the landing page as an exchange with users. You give them content for free such as a white paper, report, infographic, video, or data. In return, users give you their contact information, company information, and other business-related information.

I encourage you to think beyond this simple transaction formula. Think of your users as being in a long-term relationship with your company. This means that after you acquire their information, you will develop the relationship through meaningful, nonspam emails, invitations to webinars, and events. This way of thinking is crucial to success in content marketing, particularly when you work with long sales cycles.

> Think of your users as being in a long-term relationship with your company.

Protecting user privacy

To make users more comfortable giving information, clearly state a strong and easy-to-understand privacy policy. You may want to check with your legal department, outside counsel, or compliance team on the exact language. Your privacy policy should state that your company will not sell, rent, or give away collected data and that user data is only for the company's internal use to tailor offers and solutions.

In designing your privacy statement, note the difference between what is required by law (state laws and country laws vary) and what is a best practice. Every website must have a privacy policy agreement. Users must know that their privacy is protected and what your company will do with the solicited data. Many landing pages link to a privacy policy already displayed on the website to comply with these laws. The law also requires you to provide users with an option to opt out of data collection.

But I suggest that you create a privacy policy that is stronger than what the law requires. You want to build a long-term relationship with your clients and prospects. Relationships are built on *trust*.

Here are some trust-building practices you should include in your privacy policy:

- Your company will never disclose data to an external company without the user's consent.

- If you use an outside data processing company, that company will comply with your company's privacy policy.

- If your company is ever acquired by another company, the acquirer must adhere to the principles of your established privacy policy. If any changes to the privacy policy are necessary, your company will inform users of alterations to your site's privacy statement soon after the acquisition is completed.

- Explain how you are storing and managing the data you are collecting from users. Your answer need not be technical but should state the intent behind the data collection.

- Cookies are a somewhat controversial item for users. Some feel cookies invade their privacy. Others do not mind cookies but do not like retargeted messaging that follows them around. This is why a statement of your company's cookie practice is crucial. Explain how you use cookies and provide simple instructions for users to disable cookies if they choose.

- If you are offering a subscription, you should explain how users can cancel their subscription. Importantly, you should specify that you will no longer email them, but you may retain their data.

- You should state that your company does not send unsolicited commercial emails—also known as spamming. Should a user feel he or she has received a spam message from your company, provide clear instructions on how to contact your company for removal.

- In all likelihood, your company will alter its privacy policy guidelines from time to time. This may be to accommodate new laws, or perhaps your company may acquire another. Therefore, you should outline your communication plan if this happens. You may want to say you will email users on changes.

Less is more

With all this said, for landing pages with calls to action, less is more. Minimize distractions by avoiding ads, too many links, or too many different fonts, all of which can confuse the user. If you are considering adding other content, videos, or sidebar information to your landing page, think about it carefully. Will this information increase the likelihood of conversion? Or will it bring users to another page where they will forget about the offer?

There is a fine line between making your landing page visually attractive, informative, rich in keywords, and at the same time simple and productive of user conversions. Well-placed, high-quality graphics can help achieve this balance. Test pages with varying numbers of graphics to see which yield the highest conversions. In your test, don't just examine the number of conversions but also the quality. Are your target market and prospective buyers converting? Are influencers?

Sign-up confirmation

Your sign-up process should be designed so that prospects who fill out your form automatically receive an email confirmation. This serves a few functions. First, it will allow you to verify that the emails are legitimate and working. Any hard bounces should not be added to your database list. Second, the confirmation email is a chance to advance the prospect to the next stage in the buyer's journey. By taking the conversation off the website and to the prospect's email, you are furthering the relationship, even if the email is automatically generated. Third, you are instilling trust in the user, particularly if the email contains helpful links and contact information. Last, the email can help with spam filters. If the confirmation email reaches the recipient, your subsequent emails should also get through.

Measuring conversion

Marketers often struggle with defining a good conversion metric. This is hard to answer because it depends on many variables, including the offer, industry, and target audience. As a very rough estimate, you should see a 10 to 15 percent conversion rate on targeted traffic, such as retargeting users identified by cookies or campaigns to known users. Twenty percent or above is a very strong result. For untargeted traffic, you should shoot for a conversion rate of about 5 to 10 percent. It bears repeating that these percentages are very rough, and you should evaluate your campaigns to compile your benchmarks. The more you ask of your user (attend an event, a webinar, etc.), the lower in the range it may be. Asking users for their basic contact information to download content should be in the higher part of the range.

If you're below these rates, you need to do testing to figure out which variable changes will increase it. Start with testing offers, calls to action, and landing page layouts. See if any sources are providing above-average rates. Consider shifting your editorial calendar and budget accordingly.

But don't obsess about conversion rates. Focus some of your energy on increasing website traffic. Keep in mind that conversion rates can be misleading. It's more important to make sure your conversions are high quality. You may have a high rate, but few are potential leads. Or you may have a low conversion rate, but have captured the attention of a leading journalist or speaker in your field. You may need to adjust the expectations of your senior management accordingly. Even if management only asks about conversion metrics, as it often does, reframe the conversation to discuss the quality (or lack of quality) of the conversions and *who* is converting, not just *how many*.

13

Troubleshooting Landing Pages

In this chapter:

- Understanding why users convert and why they don't
- A/B testing to troubleshoot landing page problems
- Tracking anonymous users to identify content problems
- Segmenting specific users for retargeting
- Ensuring clean data

You can create a great landing page, but the important question is how visitors to your site will use it. Let's look at understanding user behavior on your landing page.

Visitors to your landing page will likely do one of the following:

- Scan the page, see it's not for them, and leave within several seconds. If a visitor exits after viewing just one page, their visit will be counted as part of the bounce rate (the number of visitors leaving the site after one page per the total number of visitors) on Google Analytics.

- Spend up to 30 seconds on the page and read the first paragraph or two, view any graphics, decide the page is not relevant, and leave.

- Engage with the page, scroll down, and look at various parts, but ultimately decide not to fill out the form.

- Start completing the form, have trouble with it or doubt why they should give their information, and abandon it.

- Actually complete the form and download the content.

If you are not receiving the number of content downloads expected, you need to troubleshoot your landing page. Why don't users fill out the form and download the content? If the page is truly not relevant to the user, that is fine. But if users aren't filling out the form, find out why. Is the form too daunting? Too many fields? Is it easy to spot amid all the other images? Does the text make it clear how your company will use their contact data? Is the value proposition clear?

A/B testing

One way to answer these questions empirically is through an A/B version test. Construct a few versions (no more than three or four to keep it manageable) on your automated marketing tool. Change only one variable. Choose it carefully. A good candidate for a test variable would be changing the placement of the form on the landing page. Another would be to test different text describing the content.

If you are sending users to the landing page from an email, make sure that the email list is randomly split into separate groups that will be led to different forms. This is crucial, because a nonrandom sample can create biased results that reflect the kind of user rather than the creative elements you are testing.

Other variables to test include:

- **Headline:** optimal length and content
- **Offer:** incentives, different kinds of content
- **Images:** graphics of contents, varying colors
- **Form length:** Is usage higher with fewer fields?

Diagnosing form problems

If users are starting to complete the form and abandoning it, this is a clue that something is wrong with the form process. As I said above, you may have too many required fields, and the user experience may be too daunting. Investigate the error messages as well. When the user puts the wrong information in a field, what happens? Does the user have to figure out the problem or is the wrong field highlighted? Does the user have to reenter the information?

> If users are abandoning the form, something is wrong with the form process.

These sound like small technical issues, but they can impede form downloads. Remember, only the most motivated users will persist through a difficult form. For most people, even small hindrances can cause them to become frustrated and abandon a form. I recommend that you display error messages right after the field is filled out incorrectly rather than after the user submits the form. Use language like "Please use a state abbreviation like VA." Using drop-down menus to permit only correct inputs will minimize user errors.

Garnering information about anonymous visitors

Most of this discussion has focused on maximizing downloads of content where users give their information. But the reality is that many users will not enter their information and will remain anonymous. Contrary to popular belief, you can still garner important information about anonymous users.

Why is tracking anonymous users important? Because these are the bulk of users. Understanding their behavior to the greatest extent possible will help inform marketing sales decisions. While you don't know the individuals, you can still garner some information about users' companies, at least some of the time.

Even information from anonymous visitors can help you determine if you have the right content.

One of the key pieces of information is the IP (Internet Protocol) address. In some cases, IPs can identify the company, particularly in larger organizations that have their own servers. Another key field is hostname/referrer. This tells you the visitor's origin, including its IP address and the name under which it is registered.

From this information, you can determine which industries and company sizes are visiting your site. It can help you determine whether you have the right content for your site. If your sales team is doing business with a select group of companies, you can see if any are visiting your site and, if so, with what frequency.

On Google Analytics, you can analyze engagement metrics such as bounce rate, page views, and time on site. These are indications of whether your site is engaging or not. You may also notice that users are spending far more time on certain pages. This may mean there is something to be fixed on the low-engagement pages. This could be a creative, content, or navigation issue. Try changing up one of these elements and see whether there is a corresponding increase in engagement rates.

Still another clue about anonymous users lies in the keywords. By viewing their search term keywords, you can determine which keywords are effective in driving users to your site. You can also analyze keywords used relative to user intent. Is the keyword search generally showing that the user is simply trying to gain information? Or does the search use your company's product names showing a more dedicated interest?

There are also solutions to help analyze anonymous user data. One is Demandbase, which employs account-based marketing. Its purpose is to identify, target, and retain valuable accounts. According to Demand Metric, "71% of B2B organizations are interested in adopting Account-Based Marketing."[1] Essentially, you can see if your target companies are visiting your site. The data is at the company level, not the individual level.

Targeting specific prospects

To determine the target list of prospects or clients, pick the companies with highest value to your business. You may want to confer with your sales leadership on identifying high-value targets. Another tactic is to identify what type of business is a priority for your company, perhaps by industry or by size of firm. Still another way is to use predictive analytics to identify the characteristics of valued clients or prospects and derive your list of companies that best fit this model.

You can use Demandbase for both net new prospects and existing clients. You can execute an advertising campaign that personalizes ads by industry types, for example, or tailor the content on a landing page to speak to a certain category of prospects. You can also retarget users who visited your landing page but did not download—you can serve up messaging to them on other sites to encourage them to return to your page and to download content this time. It's like a second chance for the user to receive your content.

You can also target customers for a nurture campaign whereby you can retarget them on sites and offer them specialized content, ungated content, or invitations to industry events. It's a way of differentiating the experience for your most sought-after clients.

Clean data

Finally, a word about the importance of clean data. A big issue in collecting prospect information is dirty data. If you don't maintain a clean data set, your CRM will have duplicated and clunky information, which will; impede robust analysis and use by salespeople.

Here are some tips to combat common problems in your data:

- Automatically check for duplicates. This is a very common problem, because most companies do not check their CRM data for duplicated names. The problem often arises when a user fills out different forms and varies his or her entry slightly, so the system thinks one user is two different people. See if your marketing automation tool can use a unique identifier to eliminate duplication.

- Ensure the validity of email addresses. This can be accomplished through setting up the form system to ping the email domain in real time. This averts invalid email addresses. As I said earlier, you may want to insist on work email addresses only. This is preferable because it shows higher engagement from the user than inputting a free email domain such as AOL, Gmail, or Yahoo. You should label the field as "work email address." That said, be aware of company spam filters that may block your future emails, even if that is not the user's intent.

- Standardize responses through drop-down menus. If users are allowed to enter whatever response they choose, one user may enter "VP" while another may enter "Vice President," thus making future analyses more cumbersome.

- Stop bots. Bots are automated responders that will create lots of noise in your data. To avoid bots, find a spam trap. The other option is the less user-friendly Captchas, which ask users to duplicate numbers presented on the screen to prove they are human.

14

Email

Now you have your website section for thought leadership as well as your optimized landing pages for campaigns. The next step is to create campaigns to drive interest. In this section, we'll profile emails. Subsequent chapters will look at social media, paid search, and search engine optimization.

Email remains an important channel for acquiring, nurturing, and retaining leads. Here are some best practices in email creation and subject line testing you should always use:

- Present simple messages with no more than one call to action. Studies have shown that offering users, whether consumer or B2B, too many choices suppresses responses. Users report feeling overloaded by information today. Your email layout should be clean, streamlined, and easy to digest. Don't make your user do too much work in deciphering it.

- Test subject lines. Make sure they are relevant to the content but catchy. Some research suggests that shorter subject lines yield higher open rates but longer subject lines increase click-through rates. Usually click-through is more important because an open without a click is not a lead. But if your goal is strictly brand awareness, shorter, punctuated subject lines may be best.

- Test different email content with distinct segments. You may decide to have two to four versions of a mailing with varying content. For example, you may want targeted versions for different industries or personas if those differences are relevant to the information you are presenting.

- For consumer audiences, consider asking for user-generated content such as reviews, stories, contests, and other interactive devices.

Four email must-haves

Never send an email without these four features:

1. **An opt-out or unsubscribe option:** You should have clear contact information on the footer.

2. **A statement on privacy or a link to your privacy policy:** Your privacy policy should cover what information your company collects online, how it uses this information, how your company shares it, and how your company safeguards it. Make sure to include user options for opting out of emails and disabling cookies.

3. **Social media icons for easy sharing**

4. **Dynamic personalization:** To make your emails more customized, consider dynamic personalization, in which some content is generated by what is known about the recipient. For example, users who have downloaded a report but not attended a conference could receive an email with an offer for another webinar sign-up. This can be an effective way of nurturing leads. Marketing automation tools can assist with this process.

A/B testing for email

Creative decisions will often require subjective judgments. The best way to determine the course of action is through A/B testing. Vary one item and test to see which version performs better. Good candidates for testing include subject lines, headlines, calls to action, or a creative element like colors or font size.

Testing isn't effective unless you ensure a random selection of the population you are testing. You want to ensure that any differences are caused by the variable (subject line, creative element, etc.) and not by differences among the recipients. Many marketing automation tools include list-building features to randomly select nonbiased samples.

Another element you must test is the optimal sending time for emails. You may find the results surprising. Are weekdays or weekends better? Which part of the day? During the commute or the workday? Which days in particular?

Much of the answer will depend on whether you are reaching consumers or B2B customers. But with mobile usage accounting for a high percentage of email opens, the best times for users to receive messages are changing, so testing is needed. You may even segment your list by optimal times.

Tracking email results

Once you have deployed your campaign, you will want to track it. You need to measure three main factors:

- **Engagement:** What percentage opened the email (number of opens per number of impressions)? What percentage clicked on the email (number of clicks per number of impressions)? A more telling metric is the click-to-open rate (number of clicks per number of opens)?

- **Conversion**: Did the email recipient respond to the offer? Every email should ask the user to take an action—to purchase a product, sign up for a webinar, or fill out a form and download a report. The key metric is conversion rate (number of conversions per number of impressions) and conversion to click-through rate (number of conversions per number of click-throughs). You can track this with the goal function on Google Analytics.

- **Reach:** What percentage of the emails reached the recipients? There are two kinds of failure notices: hard bounces and soft bounces.

Hard bounces are permanent. The email will never reach the recipient for a number of reasons. The domain may not exist, the email address may be wrong, or the email address may have been terminated. If a recipient leaves a company, for example, usually the email will hard-bounce.

Soft bounces are temporary email delivery failures caused by out-of-office messages, full inboxes, or too large a file size. The good news with soft bounces is that if you resend the emails at another time, they should be delivered.

A hard bounce or several recurrences of soft bounces indicate an invalid email address, which your marketing automation tool can scrub from your list.

Email tracking links

In order to track the success of your email campaign, you will need to create a unique identifier for each person who responds by adding a tracking link to the URL of the call to action. A tracking link is a tag added to the URL that identifies the user as well as other information such as the campaign name, source (which email offer), and date. Link tracking is crucial for tools like Google Analytics to show the sources of website traffic and conversions.

Through tracking and reporting, you can measure your results and adjust your future email campaigns. Which creative test versions and/or messaging yielded the best results? Each successive campaign should incorporate what you've learned for ongoing test-and-learn strategies.

15

Social Media

In this chapter:

- Using social media to promote thought leadership
- Best practices for LinkedIn, Twitter, Facebook, YouTube, SlideShare, Visually, and Instagram
- Social media advertising
- Personal vs. professional use of social media
- Using social media to promote conferences
- Video production for YouTube

The next channel we turn to is the umbrella category of social media. This encompasses social networks, photo sharing sites, and video sites. We'll discuss each social media channel and the opportunity it presents for content marketing. Some are more applicable to consumer marketing (Tumblr, Vimeo, Pinterest, Facebook), others more to business-to-business marketing (LinkedIn), and many to both (Twitter, YouTube).

One of the fundamental promotional tools in your inbound marketing tool kit is social media. Definitions of social media vary somewhat. Wikipedia defines it as "Internet-based tools for sharing and discussing information among human beings." Others simply say it is people "connecting, inter-acting and sharing online."[1]

There are roughly three major categories of social media:

- **Social networking sites:** Users post for one another and are encouraged to like, subscribe, share with their followers, comment, and so on. These can vary from more visual sites like Pinterest to short-message sites like Twitter.

- **Social news aggregation sites:** These are sources for what is popular on the web. Content is all user-generated and users vote on the best pieces. The idea is that the most popular links keep rising to the surface or to the "front door of the internet." Reddit is a prominent example.

- **Social bookmarking sites:** These are discovery engines like StumbleUpon that search for and recommend content to their users based on users' preferences and interests. Users find and rate web pages and other content.

LinkedIn

For B2B marketers, LinkedIn may be one of the most important channels, because the network is almost exclusively professional. When LinkedIn first launched, people used it primarily for recruiting and finding jobs, but today it is a prized channel for both sales and marketing.

Like most social media channels, LinkedIn offers an "organic," or free, service and a paid one. A company's LinkedIn page is the central ingredient for both. It presents a company overview, jobs, showcase pages for specialized information, and posts. Some of these posts can be content marketing and thought leadership. For example, a construction information services company may post proprietary, crucial information for the industry, like the latest housing starts statistics, or it may post a forecast for the commercial construction industry. These posts then lead to a landing page with a detailed report available for download when the user gives his or her information. Thus, the dialogue is started.

To decide which of these products might be useful for you, consider which of the paid marketing solutions matches where your prospects are on the buyer's journey. What are you trying accomplish with your advertising? Do you want to raise awareness of your products for a target at the beginning of the buyer's journey? Or are you trying to convert leads to sales?

LinkedIn's marketing solutions generally follow the stages of the buyer's journey—see Table 15.1 on pages 113–114.

Which LinkedIn marketing solution is right for you, if any? The answer depends on your objectives, budget, type of user, and conversion goals. If your target audience is a business, this channel may be a good bet.

Figure 15.1 on page 115 shows an example of a LinkedIn-sponsored posting and the incremental impressions, clicks, and interactions.

Figure 15.2 on page 116 shows some of the targeting functions available for sponsored updates.

LinkedIn Marketing Solution	Key Features	Stage in Buyer's Journey
Text Ads	• Most basic of LinkedIn marketing solutions • Self-service • Pay per click or impression	Brand awareness
Display Ads	• Guaranteed impressions • Target based on member profile data • Choose IAB-standard ad format	Brand awareness
Dynamic Ads	• Target based on member profile data, including company, skills, interests, and title • Increases followership of LinkedIn company profile page through "Follow Company" calls to action	Social media followership and brand awareness
Sponsored Updates	• Promotes posts to targeted audience based on industry, company size, title, or actual company • Expands post reach beyond your followership • Reaches multiple devices, including desktop, tablet, and mobile • Choose between cost per click and cost per impression • Make use of LinkedIn's resources if quarterly spend is over $25,000	Medium commitment: Goal is to further knowledge of products or content

Table 15.1 LinkedIn marketing solutions and their uses for stages of the buyer's journey.

LinkedIn Marketing Solution	Key Features	Stage in Buyer's Journey
Sponsored InMail	• Reaches targeted users through LinkedIn's InMail service • Deliverability is said to be 100 percent, because messages are delivered when targeted user is active • Allows for more personalized messages	Consideration
Lead Accelerator	• Retargets users who have visited defined sections of your site • Serves retargeted users display ads on websites they visit and in their LinkedIn and Facebook newsfeeds • Attempts to draw users back to site for conversion	End of buyer's journey: Users have visited your site before so their interest is substantiated

Table 15.1 cont.

Evaluating LinkedIn solutions

I recommend that you try a few channels to see which is effective. These channels could include search engine marketing, emails, Twitter, Facebook, and others. For each paid channel, you should set up the following metrics:

- **Engagement metrics** (likes, shares, comments, clicks)

- **Conversion percentages** (number of users who took the desired action, such as downloading a white paper, compared to the total number of visitors to the landing page)

- **Financial metrics** (cost per click, cost per download)

You will likely find that some channels outperform others. However, results may be mixed. You may see that some channels receive more engagement yet few conversions and vice versa. Your evaluation should be based on the primary goal of the campaign, which is usually conversion metrics.

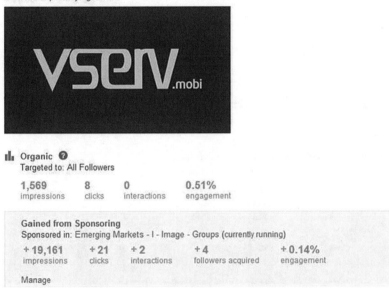

Figure 15.1 Creating a LinkedIn sponsored post.Reproduced from LinkedIn website, campaign manager.

You can find some of the LinkedIn paid marketing solutions through the Google Display Network. They all work differently and each has its pros and cons, but you may find that one is more effective. You will want to determine what the trade-offs are for each tool's capabilities, limitations, and costs.

For example, LinkedIn's Lead Accelerator allows you to retarget individuals who have visited various parts of your website. You can therefore segment users by which pages they have visited, which indicates their particular interests. Your ads will appear in users' Facebook and LinkedIn newsfeeds.

Some users, however, find the subscription-based pricing of LinkedIn Lead Accelerator to be too high. Though it may change, the current account structure does not allow for much flexibility. The program currently does not report on which sites the ads were most successful. So although you would know how many users were retargeted and revisited your site and converted, you will not get to know which web pages in particular were successful in doing so.

A different LinkedIn tool, the Google Display Network, presents a different set of trade-offs. It may offer a more cost-effective retargeting campaign.

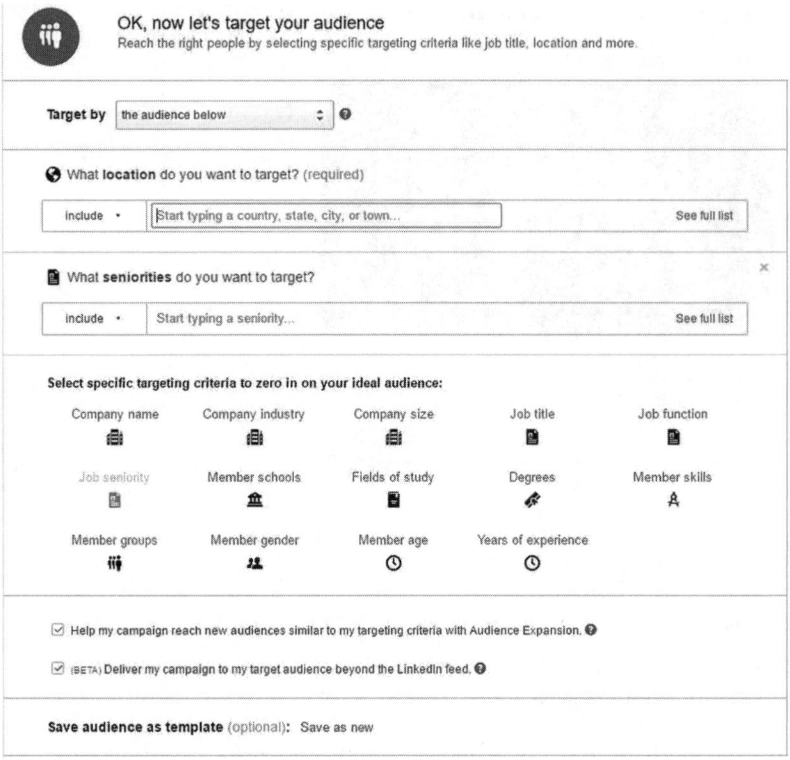

Figure 15.2 Targeting functions for LinkedIn sponsored updates. Reproduced from LinkedIn website, campaign manager.

However, its ads will not appear in users' Facebook and LinkedIn feeds but on a myriad of websites, apps, and Google properties like YouTube. You need to determine which trade-offs are right for your campaign.

LinkedIn groups

LinkedIn groups are online communities of users focused on a particular topic. If you want to participate in a group on your company's topic, you can either set up your own or join an existing one. Generally speaking, starting a new group is difficult. You will have to commit time to drawing in new users, keeping them, moderating discussions, and accepting users if your group is closed. If there is already a robust group on your topic, the better choice may be to join it rather than start something new. If you do decide to start a new group, you need to be clear on how your group is different and why it will be an improvement over groups that already exist.

To determine whether a group already exists on your topic, use the groups search feature. Click on the drop-down arrow next to the "Search People" field in the top navigation bar. Then, click on "Search Groups" in the drop-down field. Enter specific, descriptive words for what you are searching. Scroll through the list and look to see which apply.

Criteria to evaluate LinkedIn groups:

- **Number of users:** Is there a healthy number or is the group barely surviving?

- **Kinds of posts:** Are most posts job seekers or vendors trying to sell something?

- **Connections you have in groups:** Are the group's members of interest to your business? Would the members be interested in your thought leadership content?

- **How recent**: When were the last several posts? Do users interact regularly? Do posts generate discussion, or are they one-off announcements?

- **Quality of discussions:** What issues are being discussed, if any? Do members respond to each other or are they trying only to promote their agenda?

Some groups are open, meaning anyone can join. Others are closed, requiring the administrator's permission to join. Usually, entrance is not hard. You should email the administrator outlining your company, your goals in joining the group, and what you will contribute. However, some groups will have strict requirements that you may be ineligible for. As a general rule, closed groups on LinkedIn tend to have higher-quality discussions, but that isn't true in every case.

Posting high-quality content

When you join a group, make sure to strike a balance between listening and presenting your work. Try to avoid selling your product or service in the group, as that will come off as salesy. The best type of content to share is your own marketplace thought leadership on topics of relevance to the group.

When you post, write just one or two catchy sentences about why a group member should

> When you join a LinkedIn group, strike a balance between listening and presenting your work.

care about your white paper, report, video, infographic, or PowerPoint deck. The key is to emphasize the benefit over the format. The important thing is not the nuts and bolts of what you are offering but the value to the reader.

Writing an effective LinkedIn group post

Here is an example from a LinkedIn group on investor communications:

Poor post: "Download a free white paper on investor communications trends."

Reason: The post does not excite the user. It's also vague. "Investor communications trends" is a wide-open field. The best thing about the post is its mention of "free." But since this type of content is often given away for free in these types of forums, it is not adding much.

Improved post: "Learn about best practices and common mistakes in communicating investments to millennials from 3 experts. Download free report."

Reason: This post's emphasis is on the content rather than the format. The user immediately sees its benefit. There's also an urgency about it. By reporting on common mistakes, the user may feel that this is "must-know" information. Furthermore, the topic is more focused. It's about communicating investments specifically to the millennial generation. Finally, there is an authority around it. The post notes the information is "from 3 experts." The posting concludes with a succinct call to action.

Your posts should always be accompanied by images. In this case, a graphic from the report showing an interesting statistic that leaves the reader wanting to know more can work well.

When you post content, it is crucial that you tag the link to your landing page. This will allow you to determine the source of users on your landing page. Without tagging, you will not know which sources your users came from. It will be very hard then to optimize your campaign and budget.

Besides thought leadership content, you can post relevant and notable press releases. But be selective. If your company puts out a lot of press releases, choose only those you think your group would find important. It is also acceptable to mention a new product or service or award. You can post relevant jobs, but make sure to customize the posting language. Absolutely avoid a "mass-blast" feel. Just balance promotional posts with other kinds.

You can also post curated content that you think other users would learn from. If you see articles or reports on the web or within social media, consider posting them in groups. But if you do post other people's content, make sure to introduce the post in your own words. Don't regurgitate the headline word for word. Offer your insight or perspective.

To manage your posts, consider a program like Hootsuite. This tool allows you to schedule, post, and measure much of your social media activity across channels. You can customize language for each channel, automatically post on various media, including LinkedIn groups, and analyze results.

It's important to respond to the posts of other group members. LinkedIn groups are a two-way street.

Besides posting, it's important to read and respond to the posts of other group members. Remember, LinkedIn groups are a two-way street. Download other users' content and thoughtfully comment on it. You can also share other users' comments on your LinkedIn page.

Who should represent your company?

In most cases, LinkedIn groups operate as a collection of individual members rather than companies. This is by design, as LinkedIn wants to promote individual membership networking and camaraderie rather than anonymous intercompany relationships.

This means that you need to think about who in your company will be posting in the groups. This could be a marketer, but a marketer may not be as knowledgeable with the subject matter. An alternative is to have a subject matter expert in your company post in a relevant group, which will give you several advantages. First, the quality of the posts may be better. Second, posts from your subject matter expert build equity for your company, since you are showcasing your company's thought leaders. Third, the subject matter expert can likely answer questions better.

But there are also drawbacks to this approach that you should be aware of. The most common problem is that subject matter experts may not want to participate. Even if they are willing, they may post very infrequently. Another potential problem is that posts by subject matter experts may be too long-winded or esoteric for social media.

The solution then may be for the owner of social media at your company to recruit and train subject matter experts. In certain cases, the owner may post on behalf of and with the permission of the subject matter expert using his or her account. This way, you get the best of both worlds. Your subject matter expert will gain exposure and provide credible information—plus the posts will be catchy and consistent.

Personal vs. professional use of LinkedIn

Social media and the internet have blurred the lines of personal and professional spheres. Posting in LinkedIn groups is a prime example. Because most posts will be at the individual level, it is important that the poster's online presence be professionally acceptable. There have been cases of posters using offensive language or writing about politically charged issues in their individual LinkedIn profiles or on websites linked to their profiles. In some cases, clients have complained to companies or threatened to withdraw their business.

> When you recruit anyone in your company to post, make sure their online profiles are in line with your company standards.

The key takeaway is that when you recruit someone in your company to post, you must make sure that person's public online profile is in line with your company standards. This is a sensitive area. There's a fine line between employee privacy and company image. But once employees post on the company site, there is an unspoken agreement that they are representing the company and may need to make changes.

The best practice is to have standard criteria for anyone representing the company on social media. When reviewing your company representatives' online presence and social media profiles, make sure they:

- Employ proper use of brand logos
- Describe the company accurately
- Do not report any confidential information
- Do not disparage clients
- Do not use offensive or foul language

You may want to collaborate with those posting on your company's social media. You can suggest ways to improve their LinkedIn corporate profiles, for instance. Quick wins often include:

- Using a professional picture
- Creating a personalized URL

- Writing a summary

- Enhancing the description of the company

- Adding to the profile personal interests, community service, hobbies, and so on.

Starting your own LinkedIn group

If you can't find an existing LinkedIn group that's relevant to your company, you can start your own. Choose a succinct name that accurately describes your topic. Users who join your group will have a badge display with your group name in their personal profile. A suitable title, for example, would be "Content Marketers," as it's only two words, describes the topic, and is an identity users would want to carry.

Write a concise yet compelling description of your group. Use the space to show users why they should join and how they will benefit. As is the case in any online profile or ad, using the right keywords is essential. Make sure to use the keywords a user is likely to use in a search for a group within LinkedIn.

How many members should you have in your group? In some ways, quality is more important than quantity. You want members who will actively post, comment, and share. You also want members who are potential clients for your company or at least influencers in the industry. Since you will be posting your marketplace thought leadership in the group, you want an audience. But the number of group members is still important. While Google ranks searches by relevance and authority, LinkedIn searches work differently. When a user enters keywords, groups with the search term in the title or description are displayed. Groups with the largest memberships are listed first.

You will want to promote your new group as much as possible. Encourage your clients, suppliers, agencies, and employees to join if they are a good fit. Mention the group at conferences. At conference booths, you can include your group in the materials you give out. Better yet, have a laptop or tablet opened to LinkedIn. Ask relevant stakeholders you meet at the conference to sign in to LinkedIn. Upon signing in, they can search for your group and join it.

You can also try paid advertising for your group. Target users based on those attributes most relevant to your audience, such as company size, industry, or job title.

Once your group is up and running, take advantage of LinkedIn's feature to email your group members. Let members know of key updates and happenings. Be choosy about what to include and make sure not to over-email. Your group's response to your emails will give you a sense of how often your members want to hear from you.

Twitter

For the content marketer, Twitter is an important way to increase your company's influence. You can showcase your marketplace thought leadership and get it in front of the right stakeholders. Twitter is referred to as a micro-blogging platform because posts are limited to 280 characters, up from the Twitter's original 140-character limit.

> Twitter is an important way to increase your company's influence.

Twitter has evolved from a consumer-centered platform to a multipurpose one. In its infancy, Twitter was primarily about users updating each other on their day-to-day or even hour-by-hour happenings. The common question underlying early Tweets was "What are you doing now?" It was a real-time documentation of life's minutia.

Over the years, though, brands have embraced it to communicate with customers. Many use it for customer service functions as well. A common practice for airlines, for example, is to post on their Twitter page updates about flight departures, arrivals, and any delays. Typically, a company will have a separate Twitter page for these customer inquiries besides its main or brand Twitter page.

Business-to-business marketers were slower to adopt Twitter. Initially, many questioned its value and relevancy. But that has long changed. It's now a staple of any inbound marketing program.

If you don't have a Twitter profile, create one. It's free. Make sure that you complete the online profile completely. Decide how you want your company to be represented on Twitter. Most companies do so as a brand, using their company logo and pictures in keeping with their overall brand look and feel.

Users often wonder what kind of tweets they should post and how often. Unlike email and direct mail, Twitter is a constant flow of messaging. You don't have to be as careful to limit your frequency. That said, you don't want to tweet just for the sake of tweeting, so you will need to find a balance.

More important is what you will tweet. Let the subject matter determine the frequency. Consider putting together an editorial calendar for all sources. (We discussed editorial calendars in chapter 8, "Editorial Project Planning.") For the Twitter section of your editorial calendar, you may consider scheduling two or three tweets per day. You can also post on weekends and holidays and test the engagement levels.

The most important Tweets will be those that gain your influence in the marketplace and those that may garner leads. Your editorial calendar should reflect these priorities.

What to tweet

Here are various kinds of tweets to consider:

Thought leadership

Twitter is essential for any report, deck, or white paper you release. You can easily create a whole series of tweets to promote each thought leadership piece. For example, your first Tweet may summarize the report. The second can be an interesting or catchy quote from that piece. The third can cite a statistic from your report.

You can visually display information by tweeting charts. Not all visuals are created equal. The most engaging are infographics or pictures that tell a story. Users will often click on them to learn more. The least engaging visual is just a picture of the report. It's better than nothing but does not usually excite the user.

> Every tweet must have a link to your landing page.

Every tweet must have a link to the landing page containing your thought leadership piece. It is essential that the link be tagged to mark Twitter as the source. Without this, you will not be able to determine the source of traffic to your download page, which will make it hard for you to optimize your campaign.

Your immediate goal is to catch the user's attention, so that he or she clicks on your link, arrives on your landing page, and downloads your content. The long-term aim is for the user to become a qualified lead and ultimately a closed sale. That said, you should understand that not every user who views your landing page or even downloads your content is a qualified lead. Some may be media players or industry observers who are also valuable. Less valuable but more common are competitors or consultants.

Live tweeting from conferences

Whether you are hosting your company's own conference or attending an industry one, live tweeting is a must-do.

When you live-tweet from a conference, you have two separate audiences. The first is conference attendees. You can share your thoughts on panels and speeches you attend. You can also promote your company's panel or event. Retweet other attendees' messages if you like them. You can also thank attendees for attending or include links to speaker decks. Another use is to promote your booth. Be creative and unafraid to show personality too. You can include pictures of the conference or your booth. If you have a barista machine dispensing coffee to those who stop by, include a picture of that.

The second audience is your followers who are not attending the conference. This is a tough sell, because generally speaking, people who are not attending the conference may not be interested in news about it. To engage nonattendees, tweet highlights of the industry perspectives presented at the conference and why they're important to everyone in the industry. The key to engaging this absentee audience is not only in the messaging but in the links. If the links are all to the conference materials, such as the agenda, the user will quickly leave. Links that do the best, in this case, are to videos of conference speakers. If you do post a video, though, make sure you have permission if it is copyrighted material.

Press releases

Many business tweets fall in this category. Followers are actually interested in press releases if the topic is relevant to them. Topics tending to garner the highest engagement are of breaking news, such as an acquisition or merger. Lower on the list is a new product or service. You can also create press releases announcing your thought leadership pieces. Once again, you want to ensure that those links are tagged so you can measure the source of your web page traffic on the back end.

Internal subject matter experts

You can also promote individuals in your company with Twitter accounts. For example, subject matter experts who have written a piece or spoken at a conference can work well. In these posts, you would call out their Twitter username—for example, @investorexpert. You may want to encourage a few key experts in your company to create or enhance their Twitter profiles so you can promote them.

Retweets

You don't have to create new content each time. Browse through trusted sources of industry periodicals. If you find compelling reports, articles, or just insights, consider retweeting them. If space allows, add in your perspective on why the particular tweet is worth reading and linking from.

Of course, you don't want your Twitter feed to be all curated content. A good rule of thumb is to keep retweets below about one-third of your total tweets, though this can vary based on many factors.

> **Keep retweets below about one-third of your total tweets.**

Building your Twitter following

You'll also need to build your following. Unlike other social media platforms, anyone can follow your page. You don't have to accept followers as friends. In fact, many relationships on Twitter are one-way. An individual or company may follow your page without your page following them back.

Increasing your following is important because, otherwise, few will see your messages. That said, quality and relevance of users are critical. Keep track of who your followers are: which companies, their interests, and their number of followers.

You should follow as many relevant pages as you can. Do a keyword search on Twitter for your topics and follow the pages you think are a good fit. Choose a few highly relevant pages and check out who their followers are. You may wish to follow them as well. If any of this group follows you back, they are likely to be a more engaged subgroup, because they already followed a page directly related to your topic. Finding new users is a continual effort. Make a habit of following new pages at least monthly.

There are tools to help you manage Twitter, the best known of which is Hootsuite. With Hootsuite you can post and schedule tweets, analyze results, and manage your followership. Other programs allow you to automatically thank users who follow you. Many offer a feature for you to follow anyone automatically who follows you.

Automated response tools are a double-edged sword. They can reduce your labor and time. But they can also come off as mass communication. That defeats the purpose of social media, which is about building meaningful online connections.

Another feature of Twitter you will want to take advantage of is hashtags. Originally conceived by users and now a fundamental part of the Twitter platform, hashtags identify posts on particular topics. Search for which hashtags are most relevant to you and enter into those conversations.

Listening, as well as posting, is a fundamental purpose of social media. Keep up with what is said about your brand on Twitter. You can also engage users directly through the direct message feature. No one will see these messages except the recipient. You can comment privately on a post or ask a question. Another use is to provide an invitation for highly select users and potential clients to an event, webinar, or other exclusive offer.

Paid Twitter services

You can also try paid Twitter products. As is the case in other paid social media products, you are paying for expanded reach to a targeted group of users. You can select your audience for posts or promoted tweets on criteria such as interests, geography, gender, or device type. As you can see, these criteria are more suitable for a consumer brand than a business-to-business one. If you're marketing to consumers, this paid channel may be a good choice. If you are a B2B firm, however, you will not have business variables to choose from. Unlike LinkedIn, Twitter users do not usually input information like job title or industry. Twitter is not inherently a business network like LinkedIn.

This doesn't mean that paid media for Twitter is out of the question for business-to-business marketers. But you should test promotions to see whether you are gaining the engagement and conversion you desire. If nothing else, you should gain some new followers.

Here's a little-known tip for using sponsored tweets. You can target users "similar to your followers." This is something worth experimenting with. To increase the relevance of your message, you can also target by keywords in users' tweets. You can compile a list of keywords to use by looking at prominent articles on similar subjects as well as Twitter feeds of influencers in your industry.

As with LinkedIn Sponsored Updates, you pay only for particular actions users take. This includes retweeting, replying, clicking, liking, or clicking. This will limit your costs. But you are charged for these user actions whether the user converts or not. So you could end up paying a lot for users who merely click on your content but do not convert (that is, buy, download content, contact your company, etc.).

Twitter offers Website Cards to drive traffic to your website. Think of Website Cards as the social media equivalent to handing out business cards to a select audience. You can also track conversions on the Twitter platform without having to rely on an external source like Google Analytics.

Twitter also offers an automatic bidding model. It claims that the system "automatically optimizes bids for the best results at the lowest price. It takes out the guesswork and helps to simplify the bid process."[2] This may be true, but you may want to try manual bidding at least once and compare results.

Visit ads.twitter.com and select "Create new campaign" in the top right-hand corner. Then, select website clicks or conversions from the drop-down menu. Follow the instructions to build out a campaign. This campaign charges on a cost-per-link-click basis. In other words, you are billed only when users click through to your website. But this does not mean that the users are always relevant. So you'll want to monitor the type of website traffic from this source throughout and after the campaign.

By tracking results on the Twitter platform, you can identify which ads are reaching your goals, and you can adjust your budget accordingly. Another little-known feature is collecting information about user devices. This information can help you focus your efforts. If users are coming primarily from mobile smartphones, for example, you may want to spend more resources optimizing the mobile experience.

Many users complete actions on multiple devices. They may see your tweet on the smartphone Twitter app and tap the link to visit your website. Later that day, they return to your website on their tablet and download your white paper. Twitter allows you to connect these actions for a more accurate analysis.

Steps in designing a Website Card

1. Build a Website Card through writing succinct but compelling copy, choosing an image, a headline, and a call to action.

2. Target your ads based on available criteria.

3. Reach Twitter users who follow your competitors or other industry stakeholders.

4. Enable automatic bidding within your budget constraints.

5. Add the link tag with campaign parameters to enable tracking.

6. Deploy your campaign over the desired period.

7. Measure results within the Twitter platform.

Facebook

Like Twitter, Facebook started in the consumer space, initially at universities. But over the years, its reach has expanded dramatically. Perhaps surprising to some, one of its fastest-growing demographic is users aged 45 to 54. Brands have long embraced it with "42% of marketers reporting that Facebook is critical or important to their business."[3]

For business-to-business marketers, Facebook may not be the best source for garnering leads. Targeted users may be on Facebook, but they are usually there as individuals and consumers, not as representatives of their businesses. So what is the value of these users to marketers? The answer is reach and brand awareness. More than other social media platforms, Facebook allows you to tell your company's story. It allows for a voice and a personality.

> For B2B marketers, Facebook may not be the best source for garnering leads—the value is reach and brand awareness.

You can easily create a business page for free. You should use similar brand elements that you are using on other social media sites. Make sure to include a link back to your website. The page with basic information about your organization is crucial. Be sure to fill it out thoroughly. Users who "like" your page will receive updates from your page on their Facebook feeds.

Creating a Facebook business page requires a personal page. In that sense, it is like LinkedIn. Once logged into your personal page, decide which category your business page falls into. Take the time to create a personality around it.

Promote your company Facebook page, along with your other company social media properties, on your website, emails, conference collateral, and blogs. Create an easy-to-remember subdomain (typically something like facebook.yourcompany.com). As with other social media, you can purchase ads to extend the reach of your post and attract more users. But be aware that many of these users who follow your page may not be relevant. You should monitor who they are. You may be surprised to see that many have nothing to do with your brand.

Advertising within Facebook

You can advertise your business page within Facebook as well. You can target based on data commonly found in users' profiles, including age, gender, education, and languages. The keywords function will aid your targeting a lot, so pay attention to that. Like Twitter, the variables tend to be more conducive to consumer rather than to business-to-business marketing. Even if you don't plan to purchase ads, using the targeting function will show you a key data point: the number of users who match your criteria.

Consider the useful Custom Audiences feature to reach your known contacts on Facebook. This is an incredibly valuable feature if you want to find new channels for engaging your contacts. It's essentially a social-media-meets-merge-purge process. You upload your contacts in a CSV or TXT file. Besides your customer contacts, you can also use this feature with your website or mobile app traffic. Facebook then matches your inputted data against its own. The matches are added to your Custom Audience.

Steps in building a Facebook Custom Audience

1. Compile a list of targeted customers with their phone numbers and email addresses.

2. Upload your list from a CSV or TXT file.

3. Select your audience.

4. Create an ad.

Another option is creating a Lookalike Audience. This allows you to find users who have characteristics similar to those of your target audience. Targeted users are based on those characteristics of users who have liked your page, are existing Custom Audiences, or have converted in your campaigns. The theory is that by identifying similar characteristics of your key users, you can then use these to find new users who have a high likelihood of conversion. It's an old modeling technique with a modern twist.

Lookalike Audiences are built from:

• Custom audiences who matched your outside contact list.

• User conversions in your campaigns.

• Users who install data from mobile apps.

• Fans who liked your Facebook page.

Note that Facebook no longer works with third-party data providers who offer their targeting segments directly on Facebook. You can work with data providers, such as list aggregators or data analysis shops, separately to enhance your marketing efforts. Make sure to clear all necessary rights and permissions to use this third-party information. You can then advertise to them on Facebook.

YouTube

Videos are a key part of your thought leadership platform and inbound marketing strategy. Users tend to be very engaged in videos, particularly short, focused ones. Through creating a YouTube channel, you can create a space to showcase not merely videos but your thought leadership expertise.

> Emphasize your thought leadership through video presentations by your subject matter experts.

Your channel can emphasize your thought leadership platform through video presentations by your internal subject matter experts. This is a large undertaking but can be worth it. Start slow. When you have identified internal experts and areas that your company wants to be known for, videos and YouTube are an essential part.

Types of video content

Consider producing videos in these broad areas:

Interviews with internal subject matter experts on key industry issues

You can interview your experts in a Q&A format or discuss a broad question. Either way, the video should not just be the subject talking. That will bore your audiences. Zoom in on graphics to illustrate points. Show the interviewer. Shift the angles to keep the user's interest. Other video techniques you can try include adding music and using on-screen text to illustrate or emphasize points and statistics.

Videos should be no longer than two minutes or so. If your interview is 30 minutes, cut it down to bite-size clips with crisp topics. You can't fully address an important issue in a two-minute video, but you can organize a series of short videos under a larger theme. The topics you address on YouTube should match the thought leadership content on your website.

Clips from conferences your company has hosted, spoken at, or attended

When your internal speakers give talks at conferences, ask the conference organizers if you can videotape the talk. As with other video content, it's important to edit a conference speech to make it engaging. First, an hour-long talk should be edited into short segments. Don't feel you have to show the whole speech, just highlight the key points. In essence, a good video edit does the work for the viewer. You may also consider summarizing the salient takeaways at the end of the video. Conference panel discussions also make for good video content, but make sure that all participants on the panel are OK with your filming them.

Product, service, or solution demonstrations

This is where the cliché "a picture is worth a thousand words" comes true. Consider filming how-to videos for your key solutions. Be creative. Sometimes, animation works well. Or you can dramatize fictional characters solving their business problems by using your solutions.

It's crucial, however, to separate product demonstration videos from thought leadership videos. You have to preserve a firewall between videos that are objective perspectives

> It's crucial to separate product demonstration videos from thought leadership videos.

on the industry and ones that explicitly promote your product. This is a very important point. Any confusion between your thought leadership content and your sales content will damage the credibility of your thought leadership.

Keep this separation in mind not only for the presentation of your videos but for the content as well. Your interview on "Perspectives on Communicating Investments to Millennials" should not offer a few ideas and then explicitly sell an investor software solution. It's OK to recommend general solutions, but once your subjects promote a particular brand, they lose their perceived objectivity.

Showcasing your brand

You may want to produce a video about your company, what it does, and why it is distinctive from competitors. If you create a company profile video, make sure that you are using all brand elements correctly. If your company (or your client, if you are an agency) has a brand team, you should consult with it. A best practice with this type of video is employing *proof points*, which are statistics or facts to back up claims. Proof points substantiate your video, but make sure your facts are correct. Keep your sources and calculations in case you need them.

Case studies

You can interview clients on their experiences in using your products or solutions. But keep in mind the importance of maintaining your perceived objectivity, and make sure that the video is not just an advertisement for your company. Try to delve deep into your client's objectives and issues and every approach the client used to solve them, not just your company's solution. Think of this kind of video more as a small, real-life Harvard Business School case study than an excuse for your client to give kudos to your firm. It also helps to interview various stakeholders in the firm rather than just one subject. This gives your video variety and substance.

Perspectives from your clients

A perspective video differs from a case study in that your clients need not bring up your company at all. Instead, your clients offer insights into the industry, relating their experiences and viewpoints that can help others solve their business issues.

Producing videos

You may be wondering how you can produce professional-quality videos. You don't have to spend a lot of money in today's production environment.

> You don't have to spend a lot of money to produce professional-quality videos.

You can hire freelance producers and editors for reasonable prices. You could also shoot the videos yourself. Each generation of smartphones has improved photo- and video-taking capabilities. Shooting your videos yourself is a start, but the results may not look as professional as you would like. As noted above, you want to avoid just filming your subjects. You want to change the angles and add graphics. That's where a video production specialist can help. Hiring a competent outside editor is also useful.

Presenting your videos on YouTube

Once you have a library of videos, create a framework for how they will be displayed on your YouTube channel. You should use the same topic categories that you use to organize your thought leadership content on your own website.

Now you need to fill out your YouTube channel profile. Make sure you have a link to your website and other social media sources. Upload a cover picture. The tricky part of doing this is finding a suitable on-brand image that fits.

Now that you have your channel completed, you are ready to promote it. You can use other social media channels to drive users to it. You can best accomplish this by creating posts for each social media channel you use about a key fact, insight or perspective addressed in your video. You can also direct users to your YouTube channel from your website and blog.

Linking to videos on your YouTube channel from external sources is an annoyance for users, though. YouTube offers a convenient feature to embed videos within a web page so that users need not go to the YouTube site to view them. This creates a more seamless experience for the user, which means more people will bother to watch your video content. Leverage this feature to add the video to your blog too.

Another way users will find your videos is through YouTube's search function, so make sure to give your videos catchy titles and descriptions that include keywords.

Paid YouTube options

There are also—as you might expect—paid YouTube features. As with ads on other social media platforms, you have control over your daily budget for paid YouTube promotions. Costs are applied on a user-engagement model, so you pay only when a user interacts with your ad. When users decide to skip your ads, you do not pay.

There are various kinds of YouTube ads:

Skippable in-stream ads

In-stream ads are probably the most popular YouTube ads. These video ads try to attract the viewer's attention within the first five seconds. At that point, users decide whether to continue watching or click the Skip Ad button. Advertisers are charged on a cost-per-view basis, but there is no charge unless the ad plays more than 30 seconds, so advertisers do not have to pay for uninterested audiences who skip the ad. If your video is less than 30 seconds and the user watches it, you'll also be charged. You have the option of bidding, which allows you pay for every thousand impressions. Generally speaking, paying by the number of 30-second views is a better value.

In-stream ads can be an effective way to promote your content through video. The link in your video ad takes users to your landing page, where you can convert them to download your report, white paper, or infographic or to attend a webinar or conference.

In-stream ads will give you more reach than other YouTube advertising. You can also target your ad to viewers most likely to be interested in it. Your video may play on YouTube watch pages, videos on partner sites, and apps in the Display Network.

You can also target users who have searched for keywords applicable to your video, viewed other videos or channels with similar topics, or visited relevant websites.

Non-skippable in-stream ads

These work the same way as skippable in-stream ads, except with the difference implied in the name—viewers cannot skip the ad. Your video must be a crisp 15 seconds or less. You pay a fee for every thousand impressions. This option will likely be more costly but is a method for reinforcing your brand messaging. However, if you use non-skippable in-stream ads, be sure to precisely target your YouTube audience, or you'll spend money on irrelevant impressions.

Discovery ads

These ads are more subtle on the page than in-stream ads. Your ad will have a thumbnail image with limited text to invite users to watch the video. These small ads will appear on YouTube search results, alongside related YouTube videos, and on the YouTube mobile home page.

The goal is that as viewers look for content related to the video they are watching, they will see and click on your video. Note that your ad will compete with many others below or above it. Users may not take the time to read all the ads. Your thumbnail video image, title, and text will be crucial to attracting the viewer's click.

You can link these discovery ads to your YouTube channel, but you cannot directly link them to your external landing page. Users first have to go through your YouTube channel, because YouTube wants to keep users in the YouTube ecosystem.

Discovery ads are a good choice if you want to build your YouTube channel subscription or to increase engagement with your videos. However, if your primary goal is driving users to your landing page, these ads are not the best option. Plus, you may not get the reach that in-stream ads offer. You pay for discovery ads when users click on your thumbnail ad, so it's important that your thumbnail ad makes it clear who will benefit from watching the video—vague thumbnail ads will attract expensive views from users who aren't serious prospects.

Bumper ads

As the name implies, bumper ads are six-second or shorter videos that play before, during, or after another video. Viewers must watch the entire six seconds. Like other kinds of ads, bumper ads can appear in YouTube videos, partner sites, and on apps on the Google Display Network. You are charged for every thousand impressions. This option is not the best for B2B, because it's hard to design a compelling message in a few seconds for a complex product. You also run the risk of your bumper video being shown to many uninterested or irrelevant users, particularly if you're advertising a niche product or service.

There are also mobile-only ads for tablets and smartphones. However, these ads are displayed only on partner sites and the Google Display Network apps. You will pay for every thousand impressions. Importantly, this option does offer YouTube as a placement for your video. If your goal is to drive usage exclusively or primarily for mobile users using non-YouTube site platforms, inquire about this option.

A gold box with the word "Ad" denotes that it is a paid ad. You can link directly to your landing page. The website Digitalmarketer.com notes that it is a best practice to give your landing page the same "look and feel as the content on YouTube to preserve the 'scent' from ad to conversion page."[4]

In-search ads are best if you want to increase views on your YouTube channel at a lower cost than in-stream ads. As with all ad platforms, you must have a compelling call to action in the video, an attractive thumbnail image, and a captivating headline.

You can also analyze engagement on the YouTube platform. For each video, you can see the number of views, likes, shares, comments, and clicks. You can also track the number of subscribers. If you measure conversion on an off-platform page, like your landing page, you'll need to create a tag for the link to track it.

Visual communications

There is a centuries-old debate about which is more effective—the word or the image. Poets may disagree with painters. But for promoting your thought leadership, visuals are essential, for several reasons. First, images attract the user's eye in a space that has tons of images competing for the user's limited attention. Second, visuals can explain a concept or story in a more natural way, which has given rise to the popular infographic format. Finally, visuals work well with how many users read the internet. Users often don't read in a linear way. They scan key places on a page looking for information and clicking on what interests them, and images help guide them.

SlideShare

Owned by LinkedIn, SlideShare is one of the more well-known visual communications platforms. It serves as a repository for various content ranging from PowerPoint decks to webinars to infographics. SlideShare also offers a lead-generation feature, in which users can input their information to see gated content. This information can then feed into an automated marketing database.

Visually

Infographics have become very popular. They tell a story behind figures in a visually compelling and sharp way. The noted book *Inbound Marketing: Attract, Engage and Delight Customers Online* describes Visually as "both a marketplace that matches companies with data visualization professionals (to produce infographics, videos, interactive content, and presentations) as well as a visual storytelling community, where this type of content can be published, discovered, discussed and shared."[5] One example of visual storytelling is "We Are Afghan Women: Voices of Hope" sponsored by the George W. Bush Presidential Center. Through animated images and music, it portrays the journey to freedom of many Afghan women since the collapse of the Taliban.

If you need to hire outside freelancers to help you construct visual material, this site provides a worthy solution. It's like a one-stop shop for all your visual needs. Visually's design service specializes in this work, which can be hard to find in the general freelance or even employee marketplace.

It's also worth browsing through images for ideas. You can also share your visual content on this platform. Given Visually's high authority within Google due to the high number of incoming links, your content will likely rank much higher in Google search results. The platform also allows for embedding, an attractive feature for writers who can put the content right into their material. If they were not able to embed, writers, bloggers, and journalists might shy away from linking to this site, because that would take users away from their site.

Instagram

Launched in 2010, Instagram has become one of the most popular social media photo-sharing sites for users under the age of 35. Created largely for mobile devices, the app allows users to take pictures, edit them with various filters, and then share or "socialize them" on various social media platforms like Twitter and its owner Facebook. Besides photos, users can record and share 15-second videos.

This channel is best for brands catering to users in their teens and 20s, as they make up the majority of Instagram users. You can advertise on it or create fun, engaging short videos that you hope will go viral and bring more connections with your brand. For business-to-business marketers, this channel is less relevant. It may be better to concentrate on other channels mentioned in this chapter like LinkedIn and Twitter rather than spreading your efforts too thin.

16

Pay-Per-Click Advertising

So far, we have covered channels that target users directly, like email, or indirectly, through their demographics or industry, like paid social media targeting. Now we turn to targeting users by their keyword searches or sites they visit.

Users reading your content are looking to learn, find useful information, or be entertained. They may not have a particular purpose in mind. Social media posts gauge a user's interest and try to engage. Success metrics vary, but most try to measure user interest as shown by user actions, such as likes, clicks, shares, and retweets—and most important—whether the user converts, or takes the desired action, like downloading content on a landing page.

Google searches, though, are fundamentally different. Unlike social media, where the focus is on catching the user's attention, Google searches begin with the user. The user has a particular question or need that triggers the search. Though obvious, the distinction is important to point out, because it requires the advertiser to take an entirely different approach.

> The most important part of search engine marketing is establishing a goal.

The most important part of conducting a search engine marketing campaign is establishing a goal. Once the user clicks on your ad and arrives at the destination page, what do you want him or her to do? How will you measure success? For e-commerce companies, this will often be purchasing a product or service. For a business-to-business company, the goal may be downloading content in exchange for providing contact information.

This is a key point that marketers sometimes miss. They are so focused on their ad copy and generating impressions and click-through rates that they forget about which action they want the user to take after clicking on the ad. Some marketers say they don't have a goal for users. Their search engine marketing is simply a brand awareness tool. But if that's the case, these marketers should think through whether this is the right channel. There may be more effective ways to promote a brand.

Paid vs. free search results

Google search pages display two kinds of search results: organic and paid. Paid ads are displayed on the top and right-hand side of the search engine results page (SERP). Any organization or individual can bid for placement among the paid ads through purchasing Google Ads, a pay-per-click advertising program.

Google Ads are different from traditional outbound marketing efforts like television or radio advertising. Unlike traditional advertising, which charges by impressions, or how many individuals are likely to see an ad, Google Ads fees are based on how many users actually clicked on the ad, not on the number who only viewed it. This makes Google Ads a far more efficient form of advertising.

How well your ad ranks within a search engine results page is determined by two key factors: bid and relevancy. Relevance to Google searches is measured by keywords. Google defines keywords as "words or phrases that are used to match your ads with the terms people are searching for."[1] The search engine determines how relevant a user's keywords are to the ad and to the landing page. This is the search engine's way of ensuring that the user sees the most relevant pages.

Figure 16.1 on page 141, based on data from the Bangalore, India–based firm DAS Digital Marketing,[2] shows the various attributes contributing to pay-per-click (PPC) success.

The bidding value of your ad is based on how many other users are also bidding on the same keywords at that time. More popular keywords will

Figure 16.1 Elements of successful pay-per-click advertising. Illustration by Robert Pizzo.

require higher bids for favorable display positions. Essentially, Google conducts a real-time auction. As at a traditional auction, the higher your bid, the greater your chances of winning a favorable placement. However, also just as at a traditional auction, you can also overbid and offer far more than the value of the placement. This usually happens when the winning bid is far above that of the second-place winner.

Keyword selection

Selecting relevant and high-quality keywords is the cornerstone of your Google Ads campaign. Here are four tactics to keep in mind. Let's use the example of a tour operator selling tickets for tours of Manhattan.

Think like your customer—which categories best fit your product and what keywords are users most likely to search for?

When choosing keywords, you have to think the way a user would. Google will not figure out what you mean. The keywords you are bidding on must match those of the user's search and, ideally, words in your ad and landing page. As a tour operator selling tickets for a tour of Manhattan, you bid for the keyword "Manhattan tours" or "tours of Manhattan." But you neglect to bid on "New York City tours." Though your keywords "Manhattan tours" are more precise, you will miss out on many searches that are for New York City. Most users are more likely to input "New York City" than "Manhattan." Google won't translate Manhattan as being a part of New York City. Therefore, in choosing keywords to bid on, you must think of the keywords a user is likely to input.

> Consider speaking to target users about which keywords they are likely to search for.

You may consider speaking to target users about which keywords they are likely to search for. You can do this informally with customers or as part of a structured market research initiative. For B2B companies, this is especially important. You want to ensure that you are bidding on the right keywords for your target industry.

Some questions to ask B2B users are:

- When do you search for products, services, or solutions, if at all?

- At which stage in the buying process are you when you conduct Google searches?

- For a given topic (give three examples), what are typical keywords you would search under?

Importantly, you need to find out whether your target audience searches at all for a product, solution, or content piece. If not, search may not be the right channel. It's also possible that they search once they are further down the buyer's funnel. In other words, once the buyer is more committed, he or she searches for specific companies or products. This is important information, because that means you should focus some of your keywords on branded search terms. These are keywords that focus on your brand, company, and names of your products or solutions. This is both good and bad news. On the one hand, the cost per click (CPC) may be cheaper as the competition for such branded keywords is likely to be lower. On the other hand, the search volume may be very small, especially if your industry and products/solutions are niche.

Organize around themes

To organize your search marketing plan, come up with topics and subtopics, each with their own specific keywords and ads. The tour operator may want to divide groups of offerings: history tours, cultural tours, and food tours. Under each of these categories, there could be subgroupings. For example, under the history tour, there could be subgroupings or Google Ads groups for each of the company's history tours: "Colonial New York," "New York and the Roaring 1920s," and "New York During the 1970s." You would create an advertisement and 5 to 20 keywords for each ad group above.

The more specific you can be, the better. Avoid keywords that are too general. Instead of "history tours," use something like "Colonial New York Tours Discounted" and have the sales price in the ad.

Use negative keywords to ensure that ads don't show to the wrong people

You should also include *negative keywords*. These are words that tell Google not to display your ad when the user inputs them. Negative keywords help you save costs and improve the user experience by avoiding irrelevant ads. Let's go back to our tour operator example. Since the tour is only in Manhattan, suitable negative keywords would include "Bronx," "Queens," and "Brooklyn." Since your tours do not include interiors of buildings and you don't want users who are looking specifically for that, you can add "interior tours" as an additional negative keyword term.

Use Keyword Planner

Google's Keyword Planner will help you choose keywords to add to an existing campaign or for the one you are starting. The planner will offer ideas for keywords and estimates for how they may perform. These estimates may include anticipated search volume, predicted clicks, and conversions. Other features allow you to start a new keyword list by multiplying lists of keywords together. Keyword Planner can also help you select competitive bids in order to improve existing or new campaigns.

Google Display Network

Besides the Google Search Network, there is the Google Display Network. Whereas the Google Search Network relies on the user to input various terms, the Google Display Network serves ads on relevant websites, blogs, smartphone apps, or videos. The Display Network claims to reach about 90 percent of worldwide internet users through its potential online properties. If your product is very niche and you are not receiving much search volume, the Display Network may be a good option.

The Display Network gives you more alternatives than the Search Network. You can choose types of pages or websites for your ads. Additionally, you can select audience types and ad formats such as text, video, pictures, or rich media.

Depending on where your typical customer is on the buyer's journey, you can place your ads strategically on specific kinds of sites. For example, if your company is selling content management platforms, you could place display ads on sites reviewing the best platforms. It's likely that users of that site are already committed to buying a content management system and are now considering which vendor to purchase from, and that's an opportune time for an ad.

There are three ways to reach relevant users in the Display Network:

- **Contextual targeting:** Choose keywords and topics. Google Ads then finds suitable web pages, smartphone apps, and blogs to place your ad in. Continuing with the example of the New York tour operator, suitable topics would be "travel," "New York," or "vacations." If a user searches for best places to stay in New York and is presumed to be a leisure visitor, the tour operator's display ad would appear. The timing of the purchaser's decision in this example is important too. If the user is searching for lodging, he or she is likely making other decisions about the trip, so the ad is not only reaching the relevant audience but doing so at the right time.

- **Managed placements:** You place your ad on the websites, smartphone apps, or online videos you believe are most suitable. For example, as the tour operator in New York, you may choose to be on a website about New York events. Conversely, you can block your ads from sites you deem irrelevant.

- **Retargeting:** Visitors who have visited your website can be remarketed with your ad in an attempt to bring them back. The sites where your ad appears in this context may have nothing to do with your topic. The purpose is to win users who did not convert back to your site. But be careful not to overpromote to these users, creating ad fatigue. If you're working with a small pool of cookie-tracked users, the same users are likely to see retargeted ads over and over again.

There's an untapped online destination for your ads where you likely have the user's attention—error pages. Historically, if a user entered an invalid URL, the browser would display a 404 error page and the user would be at a dead end. But a little-known fact is that you can use error messages to display your ads. The frustrated user just may be receptive.

17

Organic Search Results

In the last chapter, we looked at ways to use paid search to draw visitors to your campaign landing pages. Now, we turn to the other kind of search: organic search. We'll look at how organic search works on dominant search engines. Then we'll briefly explore three ways to optimize your organic search results, including on-page and off-page adjustments.

Search engine marketing is defined as the "practice of understanding how search engines work, striving to get a website to rank well for keywords."[1] The adage is that search engine marketing is a *science* and search engine optimization is an *art*. While search and display ads can be analyzed and tweaked with some precision, search engine optimization is more elusive.

> Some studies show that users prefer clicking on organic listings, because they may find them more trustworthy.

When your website appears in a user's organic search results, you don't have to pay anything, nor do you pay when a user clicks on your link. Some studies show that users prefer clicking on organic listings because they may find them more trustworthy. Research from MarketingSherpa and Enquiro shows that "75% of searchers click the organic listings while 25% click on paid results."[2] Even if this proportion varies and shifts over time, this finding is still crucial. SEO is a must-do for its zero marketing cost and its innate appeal to users.

Google displays 10 listings per page in its search results pages. The user has to click to advance to the next page to see the next 10 listings, and so on. But most users will not go further than the first page. In fact, one study shows that "Google's first page captures over 89% of the traffic and that within the first page, the top-ranked result captures about 42% of traffic."[3] Click behavior regarding search ranking is not proportional. Thus, your job with SEO is to have your page appear as high as possible in the search listings and certainly not after the first page.

Figure 17.1 on page 149 illustrates the prime efforts needed to improve a site's ranking on a SERP.

Google crawls the internet searching for web pages to store in its index. In some ways, Google's index is similar to a book index, which is a list of terms and the corresponding location in the book. This means that your site must be found by the Google index. If it is not, your site will not rank. Additionally, Google's web crawlers must consider your site relevant to particular keywords. Moreover, it must deem your site *more* relevant than similar sites for a given keyword. In this way, SEO is competitive. You are competing for a better ranking with similar sites.

Tip: To ensure that your new web page is being crawled, go to google.com/addurl. This step is optional, though. You can also link to your site from an existing crawled site.

While ranking for paid search engine advertising is based on relevance and bidding, ranking for organic (free) searches is based on relevance and authority. What both kinds of ranking have in common is relevancy, which is a measure of the fit between keywords searched and a web page. That is the criteria for both paid and search, because it is, after all, the cornerstone of web searches. But in organic searches, *authority* is a measure of how valued a web page is. Pages that receive many inbound links, for example, are considered authoritative. Inbound links from web pages that are themselves considered "authoritative" are given more favorable rankings.

The algorithm underlying this authority ranking is called PageRank. Surprisingly, it's named that because its creator was Larry Page, a cofounder of Google. Page thought of the idea from his academic training whereby the

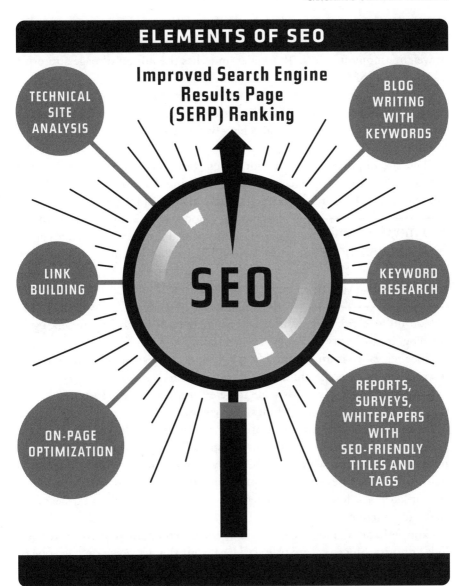

Figure 17.1 Elements of search engine optimization. Illustration by Robert Pizzo.

value of a research paper was often deemed by how many other papers cited it or sourced it. If many did, he reasoned, the paper's content must carry a lot of weight among its users. This belief underlies the notion of page authority, a key pillar of SEO.

Continuing with the New York tour operator example, the tour company writes a blog on where to find the best brownies in Manhattan. The blog cites examples and links to them. It also has several images. The blog is funny and well written.

These are important elements for a blog. But Google does not give credit to many of them. Google has no way of knowing if a blog is well written or not. Nor is it able to "read" the blog's pretty images. Since no sites link to this blog, it may not receive a high ranking in the search results page. However, eventually, particular dessert bloggers notice the blog and link to it. Word of mouth spreads, and more articles and blogs link to it. Now the blog's authority rises. Then, the *New York Times* website's food section links to the blog. With this extremely high authority site linking to the blog, its authority increases exponentially.

> You may be better off emphasizing less popular—but still relevant—keywords.

Since relevance is important, choosing the right keywords is crucial just as it was with paid search. Think about keyword selection by:

Relevance: Pick keywords your targeted users are likely to use. You can even include common misspellings of keywords.

Estimated search volume: Ensure that the keywords you choose have enough users searching them. This is especially important for highly technical or niche terms, which may be rarely searched for. Business-to-business marketing sometimes runs into a problem with infrequently searched terms. If your keywords have low estimated search volume, you will not drive much traffic to your site.

Competition: Choose keywords that are less competitive if your site has a low authority. Since you are trying to have your site displayed on page one of the search results, you may be better off emphasizing less popular—but still relevant—keywords.

On-page SEO

Besides keyword selection, you can optimize your website pages for SEO. Much of it is easy and quick, and a few simple changes can make a real difference to your SEO rankings.

The single most important thing you can do to improve your site's SEO is to choose your page title carefully. The title is what is displayed at the top of the browser window and is also shown in the text of the link in search results.

Tips for web page titles

Consider rewriting the titles of all your web pages with these principles:

- Include your best performing keywords in web page titles.

- Sequence more important keywords first. You may need to reorder your current titles to do this.

- As you should with every title, make sure that each web page title is descriptive and catchy.

- On your home page, put your company's name at the end of the title.

Writing an effective meta description tag

Make sure to utilize the meta description tag. It's an overview of the page, like a sneak preview. This description usually shows below the title on the search results page. Users are likely to read it and use it to decide whether or not to click. Keep in mind these three tips for writing an effective meta description tag:

- **Concise:** Keep the meta description to 160 characters or fewer.

- **Unique:** Don't just write a meta description just for your home page, but also for each deeper page. Note that many users may never even see your home page. It's likely their search terms will bring them to a more relevant page within your site such as a product page or resource center page.

- **Keywords:** As with everything in this section, keywords are crucial. Depending on the browser, the user may see matches of searched keywords with those keywords in your description as bolded text.

Customize your URL

Google's web crawler takes into consideration the relevance of terms in the URL, so customize the URL to include keywords. In the New York tour example, the tour operator should consider keywords "New York" and "tours" in the URL. This way, when a user is searching on Google for the term "New York tours," this keyword-search rich URL showcases that the page is likely highly relevant for these keywords.

Even better, include these keywords as subdomains of the URL's main domain. The main domain is the primary part of the URL that is on all your pages; subdomains identify subsections of your website and will appear in the URL for all pages in that subsection. If our New York tour operator's main domain is newyorktours.com, a useful subdomain could be newyorktours. com/foodtours.

Headings

Web pages should have headings to identify subsections of the page, for two reasons. First, headings help to orient the reader by summarizing the subsection's content. Second, if you include keywords in your headings, the headings will signal to Google's web crawlers that the content is relevant for searches with those keywords. This, in turn, improves the efficiency of your paid search campaigns as well as the rankings for organic searches with those keywords.

Tips for writing headings

- Include your top keywords.

- Write concise headlines, just as you would for a newspaper article or report.

- Tag your heading so that Google will recognize it. Remember, a person will visually recognize a header, but a web crawler won't. The crawler can't see formatting; it can only read text tags. Tagging provides essential guidance to the search engine.

- Tag images with alt language that translates the image into text for the search engines so they can read it.

- Use H1 (first line headline) once on each page, but use H2 or H+++ as needed. This is similar to a newspaper. The main headline defines the most important news or feature, and then there are lower hierarchy headlines for less important news.

Off-page SEO

Now let's turn to off-page factors affecting your site's ranking, which you have less control over. As noted above, the authority of a page is crucial to search rankings. Authority is determined mainly by the number of inbound links and the authority of those incoming pages. This parallels the academic world, where one criterion for the perceived value of an article is the number of times it is cited.

To get inbound links to your site, you may need to directly ask webmasters of other sites to link to yours—rather like how, in the offline world, you might ask esteemed colleagues to review your paper or report and comment on it. Just as praise from noted commenters enhances the value or authority of your report, inbound links enhance the authority of your site.

> **To get inbound links to your site, you may need to directly ask webmasters of other sites to link to yours.**

Continuing with the New Your tour example, the tour operator could ask Lonelyplanet.com, a prominent travel site, to place a link on its site to an interesting article on the tour company's site. Another example would be the tour operator asking the New York State Division of Tourism (Iloveny.com) to place a link on its site. Of course, to do this, the tour company must offer valuable content for readers.

But asking webmasters to link to your site requires finesse. Don't send a mass email—send personalized requests to webmasters. Let the webmaster know why you chose his or her site and why your content would be of value to his or her site's readers. Include a link to your relevant content. Try to avoid putting the webmaster on the spot by asking for a link. After he or she reviews the suggested content, the webmaster may suggest it.

This process is hard work. Many of your emails may be ignored or may reach the site's spam folder and may not ever be seen. So spend your time reaching out only to the sites with high authority.

Don't give away your site's authority for nothing

Is your site giving away its SEO authority without your realizing it? This may be happening if users are leaving links on your page to their own sites for the sole purpose of increasing inbound links and riding on your page's authority. Sometimes, this happens in the comments section. If this is the case, you need to instruct Google not to credit the external site for receiving the link from your site. You can accomplish this by adding "no follow" attributes. You are essentially saying to Google, "Any links pointing to external sites are not legitimate. That site should not be seen as more authoritative because of this link."

> **Not all links are created equal. Pages with few links are considered highly authoritative, and links from these pages are the most valuable.**

Not all links are created equal. Some are more valuable. Pages with few links are considered highly authoritative, and links from these pages are the most valuable. On the other hand, pages with many links have less authority and links from these pages are less valuable. Google assumes that if a site has a lot of links, none stand out as the most important.

The most important links are those that have an anchor text with your keywords. For example, a highly trafficked blog about California travel has three links. One is to a California travel company. On that blog, it says: "Learn about other California Tours." The term "California Tours" serves as the anchor text. It is underlined, and users know to click on it. Thus, Google will give this link more credit than the other two, because they do not have keywords in the anchor text.

Google views this as prime linkage real estate for the following reasons:

- The link came from a highly trafficked and authoritative site.

- The site has only three links and one is going to the California Tours site.

- There aren't any no-follow tags to the links. This denotes that the links are legitimate.

- The keywords "California" and "Tours" are part of the anchor text. That tells Google of the high importance of these keywords. Since they match the keywords for the California Tours site, this will help the SEO markedly.

Measuring SEO results

Making changes in your SEO may take a few months to show results. Be patient. Unlike search engine marketing, which shows results during your campaign, SEO works over time. But SEO efforts are well worth it, because a higher search results ranking on your site can result in dramatically more page traffic and conversion.

Table 17.1 (opposite) lists important metrics for measuring SEO results.

Google Analytics and Google Webmasters are two tools to give you insights into these metrics. If you want to correlate these metrics to conversions, adding tracking to your call-to-action links will be important. You may want

Metric	Reason
Number of pages in Google index	Shows whether pages are properly indexed by Google's web crawlers. If not, indexing them is crucial.
Number of inbound links	Defines the authority of the site as Google will interpret it
Keyword rankings	Identifies which keywords are valuable
Search traffic	Determines whether your site is of interest to users
Conversions	Calculates the goal of inbound marketing: turning users into leads and ultimately into closed sales

Table 17.1 Metrics for measuring SEO.

to establish a process for combining conversion reports (who downloaded, etc.) with sales reports.

SEO is a complex, technical, and constantly changing field. You may want to consider hiring an external agency to help you improve, maintain, and measure your SEO efforts.

18

Lead Generation

In this chapter:
- Turning content marketing leads into sales opportunities
- Evaluating leads
- How to score leads
- Routing leads to the right salesperson

Let's recap where we are. At this point, you have developed a thought leadership platform and compelling content. You have deployed a variety of inbound channels to attract users to the desired landing page. Hopefully, some have converted, in whatever way you have defined conversion for this campaign. They may be users who attended a webinar, signed up for an in-person event, downloaded a report through inputting their contact information, or contacted a salesperson. Thus, the conversation has started with these prospects, but there still is a way to go before a closed sale.

Now you need a systematic way of gathering these leads and vetting them. An automated marketing tool like Eloqua or Marketo can compile and store the leads from your campaigns. The next step is to evaluate them.

What do you consider a viable lead? What are the characteristics of leads most likely to turn into sales opportunities? The following are parameters to consider when evaluating leads:

- What is the ideal size of the lead's company in terms of annual sales revenue and employee count?

- Which industries are most likely to buy your product? Any industry verticals to avoid?

- Are the leads you are seeking primarily in the United States or in global markets? If you operate abroad, in which countries? Are there countries that would disqualify leads because you do not do business there?

- What are promising job titles? What are typical job titles of likely buyers? Are there titles that should be avoided? For example, someone in sales who is trying to sell to your company is often not a lead. In fact, the salesperson might consider you a lead.

- Who are your competitors? These should be noted to avoid classifying them as leads. Note that some competitors may visit your site, download your content, and speak surreptitiously to your salespeople, so be aware of that.

To answer these questions fully, it is best to interview forward-facing staff who work with clients and prospects. Ask your sales team about the characteristics of successful prospects. What characteristics do converted prospects share?

Besides interviewing key salespeople, you may want to conduct a data analysis of successful sales. A customer relationship management (CRM) tool like Salesforce can be helpful here. You can analyze characteristics of prospects in various stages of the buyer's journey. You can accomplish this by extracting a list of individuals and companies and entering in key data points such as tenure, title, industry, geography, and company size. If any of these data points are missing, LinkedIn can be very helpful in providing this data. However, you will need to look up each company and individual one at a time, which may be time-consuming.

> Besides interviewing key salespeople, you may want to conduct a data analysis of successful sales.

Once you have your ideal profile, write it down and make it available to others throughout your company. It's important that the right stakeholders are on board with the profile you have created. It's also important to approach this as a work in progress. As you gain more leads and determine the characteristics of companies that purchase, your ideal profile may change.

After you have completed this profile, you can grade leads according to how well they fit the profile's parameters. This will be key for lead prioritization. Many marketing automation tools have lead grading systems with a default profile that you can customize with the characteristics of the ideal leads you've established. You can also establish different criteria and grades based on different segments. For example, U.S.-based prospects may be best for companies with over 1,000 employees. Yet, for European-based companies, you may find your sweet spot at 500 to 999 employees. You will want to establish different gradings accordingly.

In establishing the grading policies, you need to consider more than prospect demographics. You may also factor in prospect's budget, the size of the deal, anticipated speed to close the deal, and any preexisting relationship with your company. For example, some companies may have been very difficult to work with in the past, requiring an inordinate amount of time and resources. This would be one reason to lower the grade.

> Consider more than prospect demographics—factor in the prospect's budget, the size of the deal, and preexisting relationships with your company

Some deal characteristics like size and specific requirements will not be known until further into the sales cycle. This is why the grades are dynamic, not fixed. You could establish a process of providing an initial grade based on what is known up-front. Once the salesperson determines the deal size, for example, the grade could be adjusted up or down.

You can also set up automated rules. If your ideal prospect, for example, is a high-level finance professional at a large multinational company, you can assign values whereby the grade increases or decreases by each data match or nonmatch. Staying with this example, if a prospect is an analyst in finance at IBM, the grade can be partially raised given that the prospect works for a multinational company and works in finance. However, if this prospect is quite junior with little to no influence on the buying process, the grade can be lowered.

Buying prospect lists

Many ask whether buying prospect lists from outside vendors is easier and more effective. The short answer is yes and no. Though it is easier to purchase lists and dedupe them on your database, the quality of these lists is often poor. Since the people on these lists have likely had little to no affiliation with your company, they will probably opt out of communications with you. Because these lists are often communicated to in blasts, the messaging is almost always too general and ineffective. Outside lists also tend to have high undeliverable rates. Buying lists can be part of your data aggregation efforts, but they're not likely to be the best source.

Scoring leads

While grading reflects prospects' demographics, scoring reflects their actions. Lead scoring increases points for actions taken such as attending an event, registering for a webinar, clicking through on an email, subscribing to an e-newsletter, downloading a white paper, filling out a form, or revisiting a website. You can tailor the scoring to the importance of the activity. It should reflect the level of interest shown by the prospect.

A key question, then, is which actions denote serious interest on the part of the prospect? Which are more minor, but notable, actions? Conversely, which actions show disinterest? Which actions show clear intention, but for a goal other than a possible purchase—for example, which actions show that a web visitor is seeking a job?

Scoring user actions

Here is an example of actions and associated scoring:

Download white paper = +10 points

Register for webinar = +12 points

Attend company's in-person event = +15 points

Opened an email and clicked through = +4 points

Subscribed to e-newsletter = +7 points

Visited site's home page = +2 points

Visited product page within site = +4 points

Filled out contact form = +20 points

Visited career section of website = −10 points

No activity on website or other in one year = −10 points

Your company would assign points to those actions it deems most important and indicative of a future sale.

Lead routing

Once scored and graded, the next step is to send the leads to the right salesperson to accept and then act on the lead. The process needs to be automated and consistent. Marketing automation tools integrated with a CRM tool like Salesforce can effectively route leads. Rules can be set by which prospects reaching a threshold score or grade are assigned to a salesperson based on how the sales team is organized, whether by territory, seniority, industry, or other dividing criteria. Some companies may divide reps by workload. Those with availability receive the next lead. Some marketing automation tools can notify salespeople when a lead is available.

In routing leads, you want to build into the process a chance for salespeople to accept or reject leads. There may be reasons unknown to marketing why certain leads are not viable. Ideally, there should be a feedback loop between marketing and sales. As salespeople reject various leads, they should enter a reason in the appropriate data field in the marketing automation tool or CRM. Marketing should then take note of the rejections and incorporate them into grading models. Certain categories, for example, may necessitate an F and would not be passed on to sales. That said, there are many cases where marketing will not know in advance why a prospect is a poor lead. It will be at the salesperson's discretion. Furthermore, marketing should take note of prospects that have advanced well in the pipeline. Their common characteristics should be incorporated into the grading model.

Figure 18.1 on page 162 shows states of the lead from inquiry to closed sale

But you can't always accept salespeople's evaluations without question. Sales teams often have a bias of picking the low hanging fruit and ignoring longer-term prospects. Salespeople are often working largely on commissions and must perform against a quota. As a result, they may have a short-term bias. Thus, leads with high propensity to purchase in the coming quarter or two will invariably garner the salesperson's attention. Leads that need to be nurtured but may not be ready to purchase for the next few quarters will get lost in the shuffle. This is where lead nurturing and intercommunication between sales and marketing play key roles.

> You can't always accept salespeople's evaluations without question.

Merging sales activity with grading and scoring models is one way to think about combining data. As stated above, you can score user actions by linking your automated marketing tool to your CRM. In most cases, these two

Figure 18.1 Routing a lead from initial inquiry to sale. Illustration by Robert Pizzo.

systems should integrate. In case they do not, there may be a workaround. If there cannot be a native integration, try integration through a web service application program interface (API).

Combining data from different sources to evaluate leads

In addition to connecting your automation solution to your CRM, consider other ways to link data to your prospects to garner additional insights. You may be able to link many programs you use in campaigns to your marketing automation tool.

Here are some examples:

- **Google Ads** can be linked to your CRM, which can offer several useful pieces of information. First, prospects coming from search likely know less about your company, particularly if the keywords didn't include brand names. This means that the user entered keywords like "expense management solutions" rather than the name of a particular product, like "Concur Expense." Usually, in these cases, the user is less familiar or totally unfamiliar with a product. But he or she has a particular need that spurred the search. This is valuable information for a salesperson. Not all systems will provide personally identifiable information. Rules and policies about this are often in flux.

- **Google Analytics** is a free tool to analyze web traffic behavior. By following the simple instructions that Google Analytics provides, you can copy and paste a short line of JavaScript code into the source data of your website to enable tracking. You can employ URL tags, which are extra characters appended to an URL to identify the source among other fields. These tags will allow you to track sources of website visitors. For example, how many visits to a particular page were from a particular email campaign?

- **Social media such as LinkedIn and Twitter** can connect to some automated marketing platforms, enhancing your data about prospects. You may be able to connect your marketing automation solution to LinkedIn's application program interface to view the prospects' credentials and connections. If that's not possible with the marketing automation you use, you can definitely integrate LinkedIn's Sales Navigator into Salesforce. This will allow Salesforce users to view a mini LinkedIn profile right in the Salesforce page view. This offers additional information on the prospect's background, education, affiliations, and professional interests that can help guide a productive sales conversation. You can also try integrating Twitter into the marketing automation solution in order to view the prospect's tweets. If the prospect's Twitter platform is business related, this can be very helpful in understanding his or her needs and industry perspectives.

19

Lead Nurturing

In this chapter:
- Drip marketing
- Trigger-based emails

The question of when a lead is viable is critical. Too often leads are considered inconsequential and are not followed up on, but this often results in missing good opportunities. According to an article in CRM Marketplace, "79% of leads don't get any follow-up from sales because they are perceived to be of below-average quality." Yet, with the right nurturing programs, it is estimated that just under half can become high-quality leads within a year.

Drip marketing

This is why you need a robust and systematic lead nurturing program. A *drip marketing campaign* can be an effective way to engage prospects and clients over time. It's messaging little by little. The name derives from "drip irrigation, an agriculture/gardening technique in which small amounts of water are fed to plants over long periods of time."[1]

Like crops needing constant watering, the buyer needs consistent reminders of the product or service and its benefits, plus consistent calls to action. But drip marketing emails don't have to be overly salesy. They should have short content that the prospect or client will find useful. You also don't want to send any prospect too many emails. But with the right balance, drip marketing methods allow your company to stay top of mind with your prospective customers.

Like the drip irrigation that the farmer puts in place and then no longer has to worry about, the best part of a drip marketing campaign is its automation. You can plan the content for each email over many months at the start of the campaign. You may want to remind prospects and clients of various events, webinars, trade shows, or industry-related news. Think of drip marketing

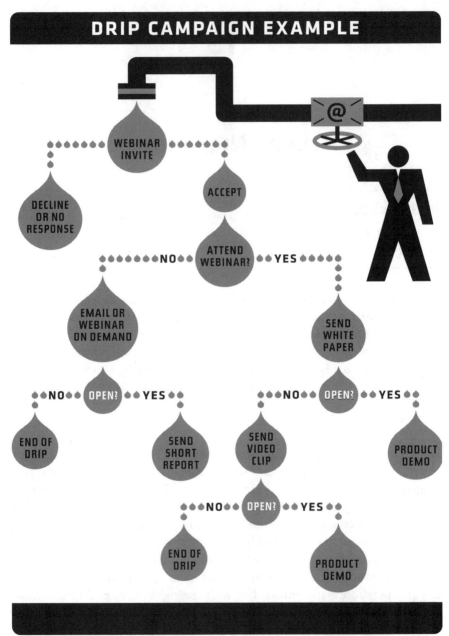

Figure 19.1 Example of a drip marketing campaign. Illustration by Robert Pizzo.

campaigns as staying in touch. From the prospect's perspective, it feels less pressuring than sales calls. You should follow these best practices with drip marketing:

- Always give users a chance to unsubscribe or to opt out.

- Do not send more than one email per week to the same user.

- Make sure each email has substance and is not hitting the user over the head with a sales pitch.

- Segment your lists to ensure that users are seeing information relevant for them. You may need to have three or four segment groups receiving different emails under this program. This is true for versioning product information as well as invitations to webinars and events.

Market research companies report that drip marketing campaigns have been successful. Forrester Research notes that "companies that excel at drip marketing raise their win rates by 7% and have sales representatives who make quota 9% more often. Additionally, prospects and customers who receive drip marketing messages buy more, require less discounting and have shorter sales cycles than those who were not part of a drip campaign."[2]

Trigger-based emails

You can also create trigger-based emails to nurture leads. For example, if a prospect fills in fields on a landing page to download a white paper, he or she will receive an email with a link to the report. But let's suppose the prospect never opens that email. This would be a trigger to send another email a few business days later as a reminder. A week or so later, another reminder can be emailed if the prospect did not take action on the first. It's crucial, though, that the second email contains different information than the first and emphasizes key insights in the report rather than scolding the user to take action. Weeks later, you can send an email of related material—perhaps an associated infographic, summary report, or PowerPoint slides.

Here's another example of a trigger email: if a prospect signs up for an event, a pre-event email can list key speakers, their presentation topics, and notable attributes of the conference. It can also include links to Twitter handles, Facebook pages, or LinkedIn group pages related to the conference. After the conference, trigger emails can thank attendees for coming and also contain video segments from conference speakers. It can also link to the website to continue the prospect's buyer journey.

20

Sales and Marketing Systems

In this chapter:

- Tools to automate marketing:
  - Customer relations management (CRM)
  - Marketing automation solutions
  - Content management systems (CMS)
  - Sales force automation
  - Web analytics tools
  - Bid management software
- Collaborating with and enabling sales staff

In the last chapter, we discussed how to track, grade, score, and nurture leads from your content marketing programs. Now we will turn to how to route leads effectively to sales teams. We'll look at six types of tools, including Customer Relationship Management (CRM), marketing automation solutions, web analytics tools, and others. We'll then discuss key sales enablement tactics.

Several tools are needed for a robust content, lead automation, and sales pipeline process. The key to getting the most benefit from these tools is linking multiple systems. It is imperative when selecting tools that each system integrates with the other. It takes a large chain of interconnected tools to achieve automation.

Six marketing and sales tools

Customer relationship management

Customer relationship management (CRM) refers to managing a customer database. The database describes prospects and customers so that salespeople and support staff can create segments, identify prospects with various criteria, and update customer information as needed. In many companies, this tool is an archive for customer actions, so that client-facing employees can see account histories and make decisions on offers, messages, and service to clients.

There are two major types of CRM. One is an enterprise-wide solution such as SAP or Oracle PeopleSoft. These tend to be very extensive systems that underlie many departments' infrastructures. The other is Software as a Service (SaaS) from on-demand vendors like Salesforce.com. The latter is where the industry is headed, due to its lower cost, easier implementation, greater mobile adaptability, and remote accessibility.

Marketing automation solutions

Like CRM, marketing automation solutions typically include a database of prospects but also offer advanced features for actually marketing to them, including email marketing, lead scoring, lead grading, tracking known and anonymous visitors, return-on-investment calculations, and rudimentary landing page building. Oracle's Eloqua and Marketo are the current industry leaders.

Do you need both a CRM and a marketing automation solution? Yes and no. For a small business with a limited budget, a marketing automation tool may be sufficient. A larger company with a diverse global sales force usually needs a CRM to provide central access to detailed information about prospects.

If you use both a CRM and a marketing automation solution, it is crucial that they integrate with each other. Scores and grades that your marketing automation solution assigns to leads should be shared with your CRM and other sales tools. So if you buy only a marketing solution now but may want to buy a CRM down the road, you should choose a marketing solution that will integrate with your future CRM tool.

Content management systems

Content management systems (CMSs) are the backbone of content storage and organization. Before these systems became prominent, companies would often have to pay vendors to make relatively minor tweaks to content on their websites. Now, companies are maintaining content themselves, eliminating the cost and hassle of using an agency to manage their websites.

The CMS serves as the repository for all website or mobile data, including reports, press releases, white papers, product information, and much more.

The key to using a CMS effectively is structuring the content in intuitive ways for internal users to manage. Often the CMS structure will parallel the categories of the website or mobile app. This way, a user can easily make any changes to the desired area.

Content management systems deploy campaigns across various channels, including print, email, retargeting, social media, and the web. Most can schedule campaigns and execute them, relieving much of the tedious labor involved. Importantly, a CMS stores content that you can mix and match to tailor marketing messaging. Advanced features include forms management, landing page building, and file hosting.

Sales force automation

Sales force automation (SFA) systems—usually included as part of the larger CRM system—organize and streamline the sales documenting process. Since keeping track of contacts with clients is the most important need of most salespeople, SFA systems track communications and follow-ups. Sales management software is notorious for duplicating data, owing to the same contact having several different addresses, emails, or companies associated with them. Duplication always gets worse over time, as different salespeople enter slightly different information for the same prospects. A good SFA system will automatically dedupe contacts.

Web analytics tools

Web analytics tools measure marketing activity, page traffic, and the effectiveness of campaigns across channels. They provide metrics such as the demographics of website visitors, pages viewed, sources of web traffic, time on site and on various pages, popular keywords, and much more. However, in order to protect privacy, these tools will provide only aggregated data, not data on individual users.

The most famous free web analytics tool is Google Analytics. The tool offers a bird's-eye view into key web user groups' demographics, actions, and more. Google also offers more advanced packages for fees. Other vendors include Omniture, Coremetrics, and Webtrends.

Bid management software

Bid management software is used for organizing and running paid searches across key search engines, including Google, Bing, and Yahoo. As we noted in chapter 16, "Pay-Per-Click Advertising," in search engine marketing, there are two drivers of rankings: relevancy of keywords to text and bidding. Bid management software automates the bidding process. Bid management software can interface with the major search engines to determine keyword clicks, conversion points, costs per click, and more. Some examples of bid management systems are Kenshoo, Marin, Acquisio, and DoubleClick Search. These systems include such features as optimizing budgets into online ads, customer targeting, keyword selection, and campaign result reporting. The advantage of bid management systems is that they work with multiple search engines, unlike Google Ads, which is for Google only.

Table 20.1 below summarizes these six tools and their applications:

Tool	Use	Examples
Customer relationship management	Contains repository of customer and prospect profiles and account histories	Salesforce, SAP, Microsoft Dynamics, NetSuite
Marketing automation	Offers features to market to prospects, including email marketing, lead scoring, lead grading, and ROI calculations	Eloqua, Marketo, HubSpot, Pardot, ActiveCampaign, Adobe Campaign
Content management system	Enables users to change websites' content robustly and often more cheaply than using an outside party to update the website	Drupal, Magento, Joomla!, eZ Platform, Squarespace, WordPress
Web analytics	Measures page traffic, sources, campaign, user engagement and more	Google Analytics, Omniture, Coremetrics, Webtrends
Bid management	Manages paid search campaigns across search engines to determine and execute optimum bidding strategies	Kenshoo, Marin, Acquisio, DoubleClick Search

Table 20.1 Applications of marketing and sales tools.

Sales enablement tactics

Having the right tools, though, is only part of the equation. You also want to ensure the best working relationship between sales and marketing. This is crucial to make content and marketing automation work. Historically, there has been friction between these two groups. Marketing often feels underappreciated for its hard work in promoting the brand, designing the website, executing campaigns, and generating leads. For its part, sales often feels it is the revenue-generating arm of the company and therefore deserves more attention. For example, sales may want more high-quality leads, or sales may not see the impact of content on its sales process.

Demand generation through marketing automation carries the potential to improve this relationship. As a Forrester Research report puts it:

"Bickering between sales and marketing over lead quality and sales' responsiveness to marketing-generated demand ends when firms implement LMA (lead management automation) technology. The routing, monitoring, and reporting features let marketers demonstrate the team's impact on sales pipelines and show how marketing activity makes the sales process more efficient."[1]

> "Lead management automation lets marketers demonstrate their impact on sales pipelines."

A productive collaboration exercise with sales and marketing is to build a marketing funnel with agreed-upon definitions. What defines a prospect versus a lead? When is a lead qualified? What are the stages of an opportunity?

As summarized in Table 20.2 on page 174, this discussion can be guided by the classic buyer's funnel. Your inbound channels, like social media and events, and outbound marketing, like advertising and search efforts, will bring in both known and unknown users. These are *general interest pursuers*. Some will advance down the funnel; others will not. Your job at this collaboration meeting is to determine what qualifies someone to move down the funnel or who converted to a *lead*. It should be someone who has a reasonable chance of becoming a client. The subsequent stage of *serious buyer* indicates a more committed purchaser with a demonstrated interest. One criterion to define interest could be a prospect taking a defined action, like speaking with a salesperson or attending a pitch meeting. The final step is becoming a client. This criterion is more straightforward. It requires a commitment to purchase or an actual purchase.[2]

Type of User	Qualifying Actions
General-interest pursuers	Converted on landing page (downloaded, gave contact information, etc.)
Lead	Completes another action like attending an event or webinar or revisiting site. Title, company, and industry of user indicates that the prospect may turn into a sale
Serious buyer	Takes an action signifying serious commitment such as meeting with salesperson, attending a pitch, etc.
Paying client	Commits to purchasing product or service

Table 20.2 Defining prospects and leads.

Using sales funnel analysis to troubleshoot marketing problems

Once you have the definitions established, you should measure what percentage of your database is in which category. You should report on shifts between categories, on either a weekly or monthly basis. Note where most "leakage" is occurring—that is, at which stage are most users not advancing? This is an important question, because it can diagnose what may be wrong. If most are not advancing to the lead stage, this could mean your visitors are irrelevant to your product or solution. You may need to rework your targeting. If this is the case, you should do a root cause analysis to see which sources are bringing the best and worst leads and shift your budget accordingly. For example, certain content types may be garnering the wrong leads. You should share these findings with sales and invite its input.

Leads who don't advance to become serious buyers can indicate a problem in nurture campaigns. If you are bringing in potentially interested buyers, but they are not staying, you may want to revisit your marketing campaigns to these segments. Are you contacting them enough? Is your marketing content personalized enough? How can you improve your approach to these leads?

If customers are not advancing from serious buyer to paying client, there may be an issue with the sales process, such as a lack of follow-up at the serious buyer stage. As stated previously, a common problem is for salespeople to ignore prospects with high potential but no short-term sales. They are working against their quotas and for their commissions. You may want to suggest a pipeline analysis to determine where additional sales efforts should be placed.

This funnel analysis can also help you determine your return on investment per channel. You can look at activity at each stage of the funnel by the source. You can then assign a cost per lead, cost per serious buyer, and cost per paying client by each channel. This will help you prioritize your marketing budget.

If you're spending a small amount of money on certain channels, this detailed analysis may not be worth it. It is useful information, but you will need to trade off the resources spent in conducting the analysis versus value added. But if your marketing budget is sizable, a detailed analysis is essential.

21

How Thought Leadership Helps Sales

In this chapter:
- Five ways thought leadership helps sales
- Sharing your thought leadership content with your company
- Creating a library of your thought leadership content

In the last chapter, we looked at tools to aid your campaigns and facilitate sales. Now, we'll look at other ways thought leadership can help your company's sales teams beyond generating leads. We'll also suggest concrete tips like forming an online content library for salespeople to use with prospects and clients.

We have emphasized so far the generation and routing of leads. While this may be important for some organizations, don't fall into the trap of considering content marketing simply as a vehicle for generating leads. Robust thought leadership can raise your company's profile. Consequently, your company may be more highly regarded during the sales process. That's true of having a strong brand too. But thought leadership gives your company an edge in perceived industry knowledge. Many buyers are looking for deep industry knowledge from sales staff and product experts.

Five ways thought leadership helps sales

Here are five ways that thought leadership can facilitate the sales process:

1. Increase credibility of sales staff

Buyers feel more at ease knowing that the sales staff knows their business and will recommend the best solutions for them. The sales staff is less likely to give unhelpful and generic answers. It is said that thought leadership is most helpful when establishing first meetings with prospective buyers and when closing deals.

2. Establish contacts and opportunities in other locations

By writing about the needs, challenges, and solutions in other places, firms can establish contacts in those locations more readily. If your thought leadership pieces are well publicized, marketed, and distributed—as well as relevant to local needs—they can forge new sales opportunities.

3. Provide understandable information for sales to use with clients

Ensuring that salespeople understand complex topics and can relay them effectively to clients and prospects is challenging. In many fields, the information is highly technical and difficult. Furthermore, in scientific fields, much of this information can be found mainly in peer-reviewed journals. Good thought leadership, though, will present many of these points in an easier-to-understand fashion. Salespeople often like that format because it allows them to learn the key information, share it, and leverage it for sales.

4. Educate employees on industry

While sales is the most obvious department to start teaching your staff in-depth industry knowledge, employees in other areas can benefit by learning more about the industry in order to include new knowledge in their own strategies. Product development, for example, could incorporate industry trends and needs into future product enhancements. Finance could understand better why departments are requesting budget money for related initiatives. Account management could advise clients more effectively. Even less obvious areas like human resources could benefit from increased industry knowledge—for example, HR would better understand what skills recruitment candidates need to address your company's current industry challenges.

5. Minimize disruption from staff turnover

Another benefit of thought leadership is reducing losses in sales from staff turnover. When sales reps leave their roles, sales often diminish for their replacement sales representative. A March 2017 study, "Sales Representative Departures and Customer Reassignment Strategies in Business-to-Business Markets," in the *Journal of Marketing* notes this trend:

"Using data from a Fortune 500 firm and a difference-in-differences analysis with correction for selection bias, sales rep transitions lead to 13.2%–17.6%

losses in annual sales. New hires are less effective than existing sales reps in mitigating sales losses. Existing sales reps who are similar (versus dissimilar) to the departing reps (in terms of past industry experience) are more effective in mitigating sales losses; however, reps with high past performance do not exhibit greater efficacy for mitigating sales losses than reps with average or low past performance."[1]

So if a salesperson uses thought leadership in meetings to solve clients' problems, it is essential that the replacing rep know and use the material as well to maintain the strength of the relationship. It may ease sales losses in the long run when a sales rep leaves the company and is replaced.

Creating an Insights Library

To encourage sales use of your thought leadership, you'll need to make accessing it as easy as possible for your company's salespeople. One way to do this is through an Insights Library. This is an online destination for your content that salespeople can easily find.

To start, collect all your content. Delete outdated material. Then decide what segmentation you want to use for the library. Often, dividing the content by personas is useful, but don't use too many personas or your salespeople will be overwhelmed. Be selective about which personas are most important to the sales team. Importantly, your persona segmentation should be the same as the ones salespeople use.

Other factors to consider when organizing your library include:

- Size of prospect's business, which is usually measured by company revenue. Another criterion is the number of employees, but revenue is easier to obtain and is usually correlated with the number of employees, anyway.

- Industry of prospect, which should mirror your company's business units.

- Location of prospect, which should be defined by how your sales teams are structured. Large global players may be concentrated around multinational regions like Asia, Europe, or Latin America. Smaller companies might organize their sales activity into just two regions, the United States and international. The geographic organization of prospects should match how your sales team is divided across regions.

Organizing your Insights Library by buyer's journey stage

When organizing your Insights Library, you also want to think about the content most useful to prospects at each stage of the buyer's journey. Is the prospect just learning about a concept? Does he or she want to explore it further? Or is he or she actively looking for a company to purchase from?

Think about each stage in terms of the sales funnel and its associated content:

- **What:** The prospect identifies a key issue, trend, or situation. This is often the top of the sales funnel.

- **How:** The prospect wonders how he or she should tackle the problem. What are the next steps? What are the dangers to avoid?

- **Who:** Which company should the prospect select to help meet this need? At this stage, the best content to use is case studies of your clients. This is not thought leadership. Rather, it's showcasing why your company is a suitable choice.

Check with sales about your library organization

A good practice is to ask a salesperson to look at your Insights Library segmentation. Is it easy to find the relevant information for a salesperson's needs? Also keep in mind that some content will only be for particular locations, industries, or personas.

Within each persona, include the following for each piece:

- Title of piece

- Image: Usually the cover art works well

- Description of piece : Two or three sentences with a clear "so what" for the user

- Links: You need to decide whether to include links to gated or ungated content. There are pros and cons to each. By having the material gated, you can track who is downloading it. But since the salespeople may be using their personal networks, it may be awkward to have them enter their information. The recommendation is to have both. Let the salesperson choose.

Note: When creating links to the content pieces in your Insights Library, make sure that you use unique link tracking so that you can distinguish between downloads by outside users from downloads by your salespeople and their clients.

Communicating the value of your Insights Library to sales

When you upload new content, whether it be guides, webinars, reports, infographics, or press releases, it's crucial that you email your entire sales team about these updates. You won't want to overwhelm your salespeople, so a good rule of thumb is to email only twice a month, unless you have something urgent.

There is another way to make your content as relevant as possible to salespeople and to maintain their enthusiasm. In addition to communicating the "what" of the content piece, draw a link to your company's products that solve the underlying need. For example, if you work for a retirement investment firm, and you have a piece on millennials on how they like to invest and save, you may tie that to a product your company has on investing with mobile platforms.

> In addition to communicating the "what" of the content piece, draw a link to your company's products that solve the underlying need.

Here is an example of a fictitious investment management firm for the sales Insights Library.

- **Persona:** Ages 25–45 with $100K–$500K of investable assets. In this company, the sales team is divided according to age and investable asset range.

- **Title of piece:** "Mobile & Self-Service: How to Reach Mass Affluent Millennials."

- **Description:** Best practices in developing investing products for this persona. Contains two infographics on communications preferences of this group. Shows why investment managers must adapt practices to suit this group's needs and investment differences.

- **Image:** Cover art or small size of one infographic.

- **Buyer stage:** "What"—top of funnel for users looking to understand this market better. They are likely first searching on this topic.

- **Links:** Gated and ungated for salespeople to share in their social networks, particularly LinkedIn, and to email to their prospects/clients.

- **Product transition:** InvestMobile (a fictitious product) maps well to this content piece as it answers this person's need for mobile communication, banking, and investing.

More ways to communicate with sales

Besides emailing your sales teams, also consider these tactics:

- Schedule a Lunch & Learn session with sales teams to explain your content and how it can help drive sales and engage with clients.

- Ask for time at a sales meeting.

- Meet with sales leaders and ask them to share your information with their teams.

- Profile the top third of your salespeople. Are they using content in sales meetings, prospecting, and social media for their own knowledge or to educate prospects and clients? If so, show the middle third of salespeople how content can help them. They may be motivated by the other group's success.

Sharing content with your entire company

Communicating your content to the sales team is essential. But also consider distributing to your entire company pieces that are relevant to company-wide issues. The company intranet is usually the best medium. Ask the person in charge of the intranet if you can write an article on a new report or webinar that would be of interest to the entire employee base. If you have an upcoming webinar, you can also include a link and an invitation for interested employees to attend.

In this type of article, you'll want to emphasize not just what the content is, but why the average employee should care. You can tie it back to the company's overall goals or customer segments. You can also ask for feedback from employees on content ideas and promote your content within their networks. They may have important industry players in their networks that your company does not. Finally, if it's an upcoming webinar, you can include the link for interested employees to attend.

22

Measuring Your Return
on Content Marketing

In this chapter:

- Demonstrating the value of your content marketing
- How to calculate return on investment
- Analyzing your results

Now we turn to one of the toughest aspects of content and demand generation programs: showing their value. Marketers often struggle with defining the right metrics. While calculating the costs of creating and distributing marketing content is straightforward, determining how much revenue content marketing generates is often hard to gauge. A key question that most marketers or salespeople struggle to answer is "What is the value of a lead?" This is a tricky question and often a political minefield. Worse yet, even if the value of a lead can be determined, companies often are unsure how to divide credit for a lead among marketing, sales, and other departments like product development. The historical gap between marketing and sales has compounded this problem.

A robust and trackable demand generation program simplifies these problems. It takes out a lot of the guesswork and can provide actual data. Still, data won't solve all these issues. Marketers will still need to define leads and criteria for success with buy-in from sales leadership and senior management. What the demand generation program can do, however, is track online campaigns and link sales opportunity data to campaign results. In other words, it can show how many conversions led to closed sales or at least approximate this number. This can help you figure out the return on investment for each campaign by examining costs versus anticipated revenue in the sales pipeline.

Calculating return on investment

There are five basic steps to calculating return on investment from a demand generation program for a given campaign:

1. **Calculate campaign costs:** Add up all expenses incurred. This may include paid advertising, media buys, search engine marketing costs, or paid social media. It also can include content development costs. You should factor in the fees for any freelance writers you hired. Also, include any fees from licensing photos or images. You may also want to include agency fees, if any.

2. **Define qualified leads:** Partnering with sales, you can define what constitutes a qualified lead. What distinguishes a strong lead from a weak one that should not be passed on? This will help you separate the wheat from the chaff so you may give credit for qualified leads.

3. **Link campaigns to leads:** The thread connecting campaigns to leads is URL tagging. Every download link you use in content marketing should be tagged with a unique URL—usually the URL of the campaign's landing page with additional characters denoting items such as the campaign name, date, and source. This way, each new user who converts (e.g., downloads content and inputs information) will be tracked by the campaign that sends him or her to the landing page.

4. **Translate leads and client engagement into financial metrics:** This is the trickiest part, and arguably the most controversial. It's more art than science. Partner with the sales team to estimate the financial value of a lead. This could be potential revenue over a projected period, such as 1, 5, 10, or 20 years. You will need to make some assumptions, and those should be noted on any reporting. For example, you may need to assume the future revenue, contract value, or paying performance.

    You can break out *net new* leads from existing clients. Net new leads would be those that were previously either not in your database or *inactive*, according to your company's definition of inactivity. Consider also including incremental revenue from upselling or cross-selling to existing clients in your campaigns. Compare whether an existing client who received your content marketing spent more than a client who received no marketing. You may even want to create a control population of your client base that will not receive any marketing for a period. Compare this control group to an experimental group of clients who receive marketing to determine any incremental increase in spending.

5. **Compile relevant metrics:** Leveraging the tagging, you will be able to determine metrics from your marketing automation solution. These include:

   a. Number of new leads

   b. Number of qualified leads

   c. Number of existing clients who received content marketing

   d. Estimated value of new leads

   e. Estimated value of existing clients' spending increase

   f. Profitability of campaigns (incremental profit minus campaign costs)

Putting all the data together

A quick word on aggregating these results. Unfortunately, you probably won't be able to gather all this information from one system. In order to properly collect all these metrics, you will need to sync your marketing automation tool with your CRM tool so that you can track leads' advancement in the sales pipeline. You can also use Google Analytics to find key metrics such as number of conversions (downloads, requests for more information, etc.), time on page, number of unique visitors, and more. Google Analytics can also show you the sources of your page traffic if you have set up the right tracking, which will allow you to analyze how many visitors are from email, LinkedIn, your paid Facebook campaign, and so on. You can also learn what pages visitors go to after they convert.

Analyzing results

The calculation of results serves an important purpose besides reporting. It indicates which campaigns have been successful and which have not. You should investigate the causes behind why particular campaigns did not work. Was it the content, channels employed, landing page design, value proposition, or targeting? You can hone in on the answer by employing A/B testing. Under this scheme, you will choose one or two elements of a campaign and employ a few versions. For example, try different messaging in the inbound channels or different creative for a landing page. See if any changes make a difference in the outcome.

Stage	Definition
Open/Not attempted	New lead has not been attempted or contacted by sales.
Attempting to contact	Sales has begun the process of reaching the prospect.
Interested	Prospect has expressed interest in learning more. Full qualification criteria intent and purchase time line is unknown.
Nurture	Prospect is interested, but there is no near-term opportunity to buy.
Unresponsive	Sales has not been able to make contact with prospect despite numerous attempts.
No further action	Lead is not a qualified prospect.

Table 22.1 Tracking leads by aggregated data. Reproduced from Heinz Marketing, *The Modern Marketer's Workshop, Content That Converts*, heinzmarketing.com.

These are macro campaign metrics. But you also need to ascertain the revenues, costs, and ROI on a per-channel basis. For a given campaign, which channels were most effective? How should you allocate your marketing budget accordingly?

You can use your aggregated data to track leads and opportunities who received your content in the sales process, as shown in Table 22.1 above.

Aggregated data can also be helpful for content mapping. You can determine the best marketing for each relevant stage. For example, for "Interested" prospects, you may send more thought leadership. You may invite "Nurture" prospects to webinars, events, and demos.

You can also track opportunities and closed sales by stage as shown in Table 22.2 on page 187.

You can also conduct an analysis of content's impact on buying over a specified period. Identify contacts in your database who have participated in your content marketing. This includes webinar registration, downloads, website visits, event attendance, and so forth. Then, analyze where these individuals fall within your lead system: How many became qualified leads? How many advanced to the proposal or negotiation stages? Did any become closed sales?

As an example, let's look at a hypothetical technology company in the construction space selling solutions to allow contractors and subcontrac-

Stage	Definition
Qualified	Prospect has a need and a budget, and is actively evaluating solutions.
Presentation and demo	Demo has been scheduled or completed; working through objections and questions.
Proposal	Formal proposal is in process or has been delivered outlining terms, services, and fees.
Negotiation	Prospect has verbally agreed to do business; both sides are working through final legal/term/service/fee details.
Close	Agreement has been signed and returned.
Closed lost	Opportunity has stalled indefinitely or is dead.

Table 22.2 Tracking opportunities and closed sales by stage. Reproduced from Heinz Marketing, *The Modern Marketer's Workshop, Content That Converts*, heinz-marketing.com.

tors in different locales to collaborate online with real-time updates. The company conducts several marketing campaigns to draw prospects—contractors and subcontractors—to download thought leadership content. Leads are collected. Prospects are also invited to the company's conference. The company also conducts a drip email campaign to reengage prospects. The company then analyzes how many of these leads advanced in the sales funnel from March to July of the previous year. How many became closed sales?

This will give a general sense of content marketing's effect on leads. But take this data with a grain of salt. Many different factors can determine whether a qualified lead advances to the subsequent stages, including factors independent of your content marketing such as price, product quality, sales ability, timing around budgets, and many more. The main metric would be the number of qualified leads. Though just an estimate, this analysis will likely be more meaningful than analyzing a single campaign's lead/opportunity/closed sale result.

23

Communicating to
Senior Management

In this chapter:
- Demonstrating the value of your efforts to your management
- Metrics senior managers care about
- Creating an operational dashboard

We have talked about the need to translate your content into business value. That's one of the most important sentences in this book. If you don't show the business value of content management, your senior management may grow tired of it and not give it the resources it needs to grow. In this chapter, we'll look more closely at ways to actually communicate your metrics to management. If you're an entrepreneur, this may mean communicating to your board of directors or investors. If you're an agency or consultant, it means communicating to your clients' management.

When you present your content plans to senior management, it's essential to focus on business-driving metrics. Be careful not to get caught up in presenting the minute details of your campaigns. Most likely your senior management will want to know about leads, opportunities, closed sales, and any revenue impact. But it's important to set the right expectations too. For example, overeager executives may expect your webinar to produce a certain level of closed sales. That may not be realistic. After all, just because someone attended a webinar on a thought leadership topic does not mean he or she is ready to buy. So explain your lead nurturing process. What kind of marketing promotions would a webinar attendee receive?

> When you present your content plans to management, focus on business-driving metrics.

> By reporting your metrics regularly, you'll share the value and raise awareness of what you are doing.

If your company has a monthly or quarterly presentation for your senior leadership, see if you can include two or three content metrics. These metrics could be something like the number of net new leads created or average revenue from closed sales to buyers who interacted with your content marketing. By reporting on this regularly, you'll show the value and raise awareness of what you are doing. The problem, of course, is that sometimes your results will be poor or mixed. That's OK. Other teams will also occasionally report poor results. If your results are not impressive, make sure to explain why they may have declined and what your plan is to correct them.

Think of communicating your results in terms of a scorecard for senior management and a dashboard of operational metrics for marketers working on the day-to-day campaign.

Scorecard for senior management

You can divide your results by channel and with these parameters:

- **Existing clients versus net new inquiries:** Both are important. Engaging your clients with content is important for upselling and retaining clients. Net new inquiries would be prospects with whom you have not previously done business. These prospects may be in your database but have not responded to any previous communication.

- **Funnel behavior:** How many leads were marketing qualified leads (MQLs) versus sales qualified leads (SQLs) and then how many of those translated to opportunities and closed sales?

You can portray results by channel in a funnel. Here are quick definitions for each stage:

- **Number promoted to:** The total number of recipients who actually received your promotion. This number excludes hard bounces on emails and only counts how many were actually delivered.

- **Number of existing clients:** Of those who responded, how many are already paid clients or are close to being signed as clients?

- **Number of net new leads:** Campaign responders with whom you have not previously done business. They may be in your database but have not responded to previous campaigns.

- **Number of marketing qualified leads (MQLs):** Of the net new leads, this subpopulation fits into qualifications or criteria that marketing has established to qualify as a lead. These qualifications may be their company size, industry, and so on. MQLs have expressed interest by responding to a campaign or series of campaigns.

- **Number of sales qualified leads (SQLs):** A term often used in Salesforce, an SQL means that a salesperson has also qualified the lead and that it is ready to be contacted.

- **Number of opportunities:** The quota-carrying salesperson has determined that the lead is in fact a potential sale after communicating with that prospect. At this point, the sales process is in full swing. Depending on the industry, this could mean proposals, sales visits, and presentations.

- **Number of closed sales:** The number of leads who have signed contracts as paid clients. Depending on the industry, this could be a multiyear agreement so revenue is usually recognized each year of the agreement.

You'll want to share this executive dashboard with sales leaders too. They should understand which campaigns have been successful from a lead conversion perspective. It's an opportunity for marketing and sales to troubleshoot where leads may not be advancing in the funnel too.

Operational dashboard

While the metrics listed above are useful for executive reporting, you will also want a dashboard showing operational metrics.

The metrics in your operational dashboard will depend on channels. When drawing it up, ask yourself what you want to show. Some examples are:

- **Delivery rates:** What percentage of your emails were hard bounces (permanently failed email addresses) and which were soft bounces (temporary nondeliveries)?

- **Email engagement rates:** Most common are open rates (number of opens per numbers delivered) and click-through rates (number of clicks per numbers delivered).

- Depending on the channel, this could be likes, shares (which show higher engagement as the users are forwarding on the posts to their networks), comments, and clicks. For Twitter, retweets show the highest level of engagement.

You can show these metrics for each campaign. To go into more detail, you can test one version versus another through A/B testing. For example, on LinkedIn, you may set up a test where you have identical posts with four different visual accompaniments: photo, artwork, report cover, and no visual.

As part of this version testing, you can then report on the results by engagement rate (Likes + Shares + Comments/Total Number Viewing Post) and by comparing the number of clicks and number of downloads or conversions.

Tim Parker, partner at Bloom Group, a prominent content marketing consulting firm, suggests that metrics should start with simple measures and gets progressively more sophisticated. Parker emphasizes that companies won't measure all of these, saying that, "Broadly speaking, in the early days the top ones are more important. As the brand becomes established, the lower ones become more important. The measures for a direct mail campaign (with content) will be different."

Sample Metrics

Production

Number of items

Quality of items

Popularity

Unique visitors

Time on site

Page views

Gated downloads

Ungated downloads

Webinar attendance

Stickiness

Return visitors

Platform subscriptions

Social media followers

RSS tracking

Importance
> Google PageRank
> Number of inbound links

Sharing
> Likes, shares, tweets, retweets
> Emails direct from site

Engagement
> Comments on articles
> Mentions in the press

Amplification
> Mentions in the press
> Citations in analyst reports
> Requests for quotes/comments
> Requests for speakers

Impact
> Requests for speakers
> Surveys of TL reputation

24

Profiles

Let's look at examples from financial services, technology, and consumer retail for best practices in content marketing.

Choosing profiles

D!gitalist Magazine published a list of companies demonstrating the best content marketing. The entries in this cross-industry list are in alphabetical order.

D!gitalist also lists these criteria for excellence in content marketing:

- Defines content marketing and puts someone in charge

- Publishes content audiences want

- Publishes on a regular basis

- Publishes content from a combination of named authors

- Covers a variety of topics in which the company has authoritative expertise

- Considers whether its content marketing will be more or less branded and on domain (the same as your company URL) or off domain (a website you have to buy)

- Optimizes efforts on building subscribers or leads

- Measures content marketing ROI based on the ability to reach, engage, and convert new audiences for as little investment as possible[1]

For the following discussion, I took three companies from *D!gitalist*'s list to represent different industries: American Express OPEN Forum (financial services for small business), IBM Institute for Business Value (technology), and Whole Foods (consumer retail).

I added two more examples to illustrate other industries.: Trusted Media Brands, Inc. (media) to examine how a magazine publishing company uses thought leadership to engage advertisers, and an innovative nonprofit, the Museum at Eldridge Street in New York City's Lower East Side.

American Express's OPEN Forum

American Express's OPEN Forum is often cited as the gold standard for content marketing. This program helps U.S small businesses and credit card customers to connect with each other, access exclusive content, and stay informed on key issues to help small-business owners grow their business.

OPEN Forum was created around 2007 with the stated mission of providing "Insights and resources dedicated exclusively to the success of small business owners." Its tagline is "Insights, Inspiration, and Connections to Grow Your Business."

Mary Ann Fitzmaurice Reilly, former senior vice president of partnership and business development, noted, "We already had a large part of the pie, so our biggest opportunity was with small business growth—if they grow, we grow."[2] She and her team uncovered this segment's needs through surveying customers. Sixty percent of survey respondents noted that they were not sure how to leverage social media effectively for their business. At the time, only a small percentage of them were using social networking. So OPEN put out through its forum relevant, thoughtful, and useful content on small business and social media. Customers began to see the site as a go-to place for solutions.

Fitzmaurice Reilly described how she and her team try to see the small-business customers' perspective to select the most relevant content: "How do you align your branded content with relevancy for your readers? In American Express's case, using data to gain as much insight into the interests of our audience solves this challenge. What are our fans reading most often? What's resonating with them? We used those answers to craft relevant content for our audience."[3]

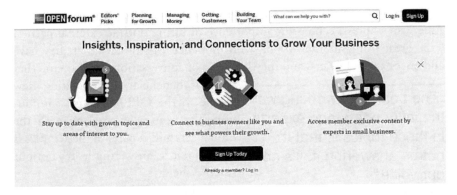

Figure 24.1 American Express's OPEN Forum

Ultimately, OPEN Forum decided on four key topics to match core small business needs.

- Planning for Growth

- Managing Money

- Getting Customers

- Building Your Team

Note that these topics don't always align with American Express's card offerings.

In providing content that small business customers would find trustworthy, OPEN Forum looked to outside experts. NewsCred and Redshift Research surveys showed that customers do not always believe their financial institutions' own writers because the information from a bank was not seen as objective. In fact, one study observed that one in five respondents "would not trust finance content written by representatives of their bank," while just over half would trust content written by reporters with a financial background.

> "American Express has learned that the only way to establish its authority on its subjects is to call in the experts."

Fitzmaurice Reilly reflected on these findings: "It's a temptation for many brands to get their employees writing and providing material to their branded content channels. However, this strategy often leads to noncredible pieces of branded material. American Express has learned that the only way to establish its authority on its subjects is to call in the experts."[4]

Courtney Colwell, director of OPEN Forum and content marketing at American Express, echoes the importance of hiring outside external parties. "The great thing about working with influencers is the fact that they have audiences and followers, and they have lots of conversations with them. That reach is beneficial for attracting new people to the OPEN Forum community. The beauty of working with the influencers and experts in these topics is that it's not us answering it. It's not our voice,"[5] she says.

> "The beauty of working with the influencers and experts in these topics is that it's not us answering it. It's not our voice."

Notably, OPEN Forum presents varying content at each stage of the buyer's journey:

- **Awareness:** Content for a large audience with broad topics. The content is not gated and seeks to respond to key questions and needs of the small business target user.

- **Evaluation stage:** Higher value content that is gated on narrower topics. OPEN Forum does this with profiling case studies and guides. They are solely for OPEN members, who must enter their validating contact information to gain access.

- **Purchase stage:** Case studies highlighting OPEN's services and products. The primary vehicle is Card Member Spotlights, which depict actual Amex card members' business success fueled in part by OPEN's products.

Besides providing compelling content, OPEN Forum also offers a platform for small-business owners to discuss, share advice, pose questions, and give reviews. Soon after its inception, LinkedIn began to take off. Rather than fight the popular site, Forum integrated with the site rather than competing against it. OPEN Forum enabled new users to sign up with their LinkedIn accounts through an application program interface (API). In doing so, OPEN was careful not to overstep its bounds. Messaging around the LinkedIn sign-in notes that OPEN "will never post on the user's behalf." The privacy statement was revised accordingly and displayed as well.

IBM Institute for Business Value

The IBM Institute for Business Value brings thought leadership, business insights, and leading edge thinking on technology trends such as cloud, mobile, and digital across multiple industries.

One of the more noted thought leadership platforms, IBM Institute for Business Value showcases best practices in thought leadership and content marketing. Its tagline is "Discover emerging trends, business innovations, and success patterns."

The institute offers featured thought leadership in functional areas such as customer experience, cloud, and analytics as well as industries like automotive, chemicals, or energy. A drop-down menu offers users the chance to filter by either. The white papers and reports are generally ungated. Report creators and experts are shown with their LinkedIn profiles. Users can download an app on iTunes or Google Play to access mobile thought leadership including case studies. They can also subscribe to the *IdeaWatch* newsletter.

Peter Korsten, partner and vice president in IBM's Global Business Services Strategy and Analytics Group, commented on the role of thought leadership in marketing and selling solutions. He noted, "We try to explore what we call 'at and over the horizon' concepts, functions and emerging themes in all of the major business functions. We identify what is going to happen, what companies are preparing for, and how they plan to differentiate themselves. We also focus on a set of what we call emerging themes like cloud, business analytics, mobile, social, and security, just to name a few. Thought leadership is trying to preview and gain a better understanding of what is at and over the horizon that our customers care about."[6]

Korsten emphasized the link between thought leadership and business solutions. He notes that companies need to think of ways to repackage solutions to make them ever more relevant. "Solutions is a good word for this bundling of value added services that allow the customer to realize and experience the full value of the products that they purchase. Examples of this today are groceries that are delivered to your home with recipes that are connected to the types of food that was purchased, or the ways that companies now provide online fitting services for clothes, shoes and other personal items."[7]

He explained that this is most apparent with highly complex business-to-business problems like those at IBM. More related to their offerings is the IBM Interactive Experience. This offers themes like "Reinventing the Wheel," which display videos on offerings along with decks in SlideShare. These themes are connected to a larger campaign. In this example, it's under the Watson capabilities campaign, which is showcased through the IBM iX Auto.

Another component of IBM's thought leadership is the Global C-Suite Study. This study asks over 5,000 global leaders about their greatest concerns.

IdeaWatch
Business perspectives from
the IBM Institute for Business Value

Uniquely Generation Z:
What brands should know about today's
youngest consumers
Read more | Join the discussion

Accelerating Security:
Winning the race to vehicle integrity and
data privacy
Read more | Join the discussion

Healthcare rallies for blockchains:
Keeping patients at the center
Read more | Join the discussion

Extending Expertise:
How cognitive computing is transforming
HR and the employee experience
Read more | Join the discussion

**Enterprise innovation in the
cognitive era:**
Igniting cultural transformation for the
future of work
Read more | Join the discussion

**The 2017 Customer Experience Index
Executive Summary**
Read more | Join the discussion

The sun shines on solar:
Consciousness, efficiency and the surge
in the solar economy
Read more | Join the discussion

Figure 24.2 IBM's *IdeaWatch* newsletter.

A common theme is surviving in the age of disruption. Eric Lesser, research director of the IBM Institute for Business Value, explained in an interview with ITSMA that "readers are looking for trusted and reputable sources where they are getting not only something of value from their 15 minutes of reading but also something that they can do something about."[8]

Lesser brought up an often overlooked point: A company's clients can also be its best content creators. This can take the form of interviews and surveys or a collaboration in creating the thought leadership piece.

In the case of the C-Suite Study, IBM leverages its international sales force to interview clients. Given the already existing relationships, this is considered a more productive inquiry. Lesser further noted, "You can come up with the greatest insights in the world, but if the field isn't prepared to address it with their clients, then you have suboptimized your investment."[9]

Part of IBM's success is that both its sales force and its subject matter experts (SMEs) receive tools to engage in meaty conversations with their clients. The SMEs are trained to ask interactive questions and build on the answers.

> A company's clients can also be its best content creators.

Lesser and his team use a variety of formats to arm salespeople for these talks. "Some people do better with infographics, while others want highly detailed reports, so IBM provides its salespeople and SMEs with a variety of materials and formats. You have different learning styles; you have cultural differences when you're dealing with global audiences, so multiple kinds of materials are essential."[10]

IBM measures the impact of thought leadership with the following metrics:

- Press coverage

- Number of speeches given on basis of content (who gave them, location, industries)

- Number of clicks on web pages

- Newsletter readership

IBM aggregates these statistics to measure year-over-year differences.

Whole Foods

Whole Foods Market Inc. is a premium Austin, Texas–based supermarket chain known for featuring organic and artificial-preservative-free products. It operates about 500 supermarkets in the United States, Canada, and the United Kingdom.

In early 2017, the company was faltering. Whole Foods Markets announced the closure of nine of its stores. Analysts noted that the company was struggling from competition and lagging growth and suffering from the perception of its high prices—the brand was often dubbed "Whole Paycheck." Other supermarkets were increasingly offering similar experiences but at lower costs. Moreover, the government imposed substantial fines on the company for price fixing and other consumer protection violations. In mid-2017, the industry received a surprise. Amazon announced it was acquiring Whole Foods Market and adding about 400 physical stores to its e-commerce assets. Amazon created new promotions to lower the price of everyday items and used its distribution and delivery assets as well as Amazon Prime to reinvigorate the struggling company.

Whole Foods is considered best-in-class in content marketing for its consumers. Its blogs, multiple social media channels, and in-store events enhance the customer relationship and seek to drive more engagement and retention.

The type of content Whole Foods creates is a great combination of company-related news and industry insights as well as consumer-generated, entertaining, and useful information.

Prior to the Amazon acquisition, Whole Foods blogs and social media sites were more store specific. Now the company has individualized web pages for most stores. These pages share most of their content but post store-specific

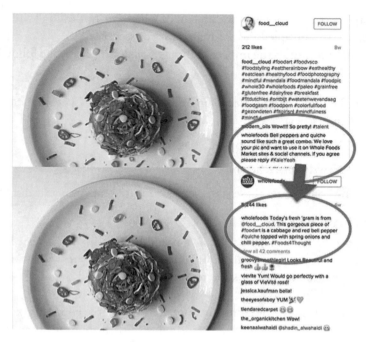

Figure 24.3 Whole Foods reuses and amplifies content from food bloggers.

events and promotions. This way, users can receive information related to their store and Whole Foods social media associates don't have to produce new content for each store site.

Twitter is one of Whole Foods' most popular social media presences. About 60 percent of Whole Foods' tweets consist of recipes. These recipe tweets link to either the Whole Foods blog or YouTube channel. In addition to recipes, tweets offer tips on household chores like cleaning. Facebook is Whole Foods' second most popular network and also posts many recipes. Whole Foods' Instagram contains photos from food and lifestyle bloggers. Whole Foods will scout blogs and ask permission to use photos. In the comments section, Whole Foods would write, "We love your pic and want to use it on Whole Foods market sites and social channels. If you agree, reply."[11]

Whole Foods was among the first brands to leverage Pinterest.

Its blog *The Whole Story* discusses healthy eating, cooking tips, and recipes without overtly selling product. Many of the stories are about making life easier and simpler. The blog's content is applicable to new visitors and to seasoned customers. Some content is specific to household types—for example, offering parents with school-age children nutrition tips for families, family meal planning, and kid-friendly recipes. There are also games, prizes, and contests. Besides the expected corporate blog, there is a CEO blog that shows the company's commitment to customers and its values from the top.

In interviews, Whole Foods executives explained the importance of conveying the company's values to customers. It is a competitive differentiator in a crowded marketplace. Therefore, content on the website, blogs, and other online destinations emphasizes Whole Foods Market's suppliers and employees. Through online surveys on its sites, the company learns more about its customers, preferences, and social issues of importance to them.

> Conveying the company's values to customers is a competitive differentiator in a crowded marketplace.

The Whole Story is known for having original, thoughtful, helpful content relevant to the products, all of which is connected to the theme of healthy eating. While articles may differ, virtually all are directly or indirectly related to customers eating better. The blog provides the "what" and the "how." This theme or social mission is portrayed not only through a series of facts but also through stories. The blog also ties this to community benefits like supporting local homegrown produce producers.

With consistent posting on all major social and photo sharing sites, the company engages its audience through "conversations." Through contests, store events, brief posts, longer stories, and executive blogging, Whole Foods brings to life its brand.

Whole Foods has demonstrated formidable content marketing for a consumer brand. The idea is "to use content to build an idea and establish a consistent message or identity in the minds of the audience. Reiterating that thought and philosophy over and over again makes it believable and takes it beyond the level of just content—it starts conversations that matter."[12]

Trusted Media Brands Inc.

Trusted Media Brands Inc. (formerly Reader's Digest Association) publishes magazines including *Reader's Digest, Taste of Home, Reminisce, Birds & Blooms, Country, Country Woman,* and *Farm & Ranch Living.* I interviewed Rich Sutton, chief revenue officer of Trusted Media Brands. The company dates back to 1922 when DeWitt Wallace and his new bride, Lila, founded the iconic *Reader's Digest* magazine in their Greenwich Village apartment. Wounded in World War One, DeWitt Wallace spent his time in a French hospital reading the plethora of magazines and decided there was an opportunity to condense articles into a single publication. The couple launched the first magazine in 1922 and by the early 1970s had about 30 million subscribers.

Sutton explained that Trusted Media Brands leverages thought leadership for its PR value and to engage advertisers for its 10 or so magazines and digital properties. Trusted Media Brands engages a research company to identify the needs of potential advertisers. The company designs questions for advertisers and agency buyers to "get at key insights and to take the pulse of the market." Trusted Media Brands then uses the findings for its planning and forecasting, to pitch primary data to the media as thought leadership news, and for sales teams to engage their clients.

Trusted Media Brands distributes this content primarily through email blasts with carefully crafted subject lines, PR newswires, social media, and most importantly, its sales teams. At regular meetings, the TMBI communications team conveys the key findings and "so whats" for sales teams. Sutton noted that live presentations to meetings can be more effective than emails: "It cuts through the email clutter," he notes.

One example of a topic is "The Future of Digital Video." The research and ensuing paper posed questions like "Which video distribution platforms are used most by advertisers?" It asked advertisers about new features such as livestream videos, "micro commercials," and the "play automatically in browser view video model on Facebook. The survey also examined advertiser perceptions on platforms like Snapchat, asking whether this was a "business model or a fad."

Figure 24.4 opposite presents a PowerPoint slide showing one example of findings from "The Future of Digital Video."

Another example is a report on the effect of fake news and ad fraud on advertisers. The survey polled about 300 agency and client-side marketers about the digital buying process. The survey uncovered the key difficulties participants have when buying ads programmatically. Indeed, 71 percent of respondents noted it was "difficult to ensure brand safe environments while buying programmatically on the open exchange."[13]

Sutton and his team provided a perspective on the data findings. For example, in the case of the fake news survey, Sutton noted that "Fake news, ad fraud, and nonpremium content has marketers rethinking where and how they place their digital ads," which is why many publishers offer private marketplaces and guaranteed accuracy.

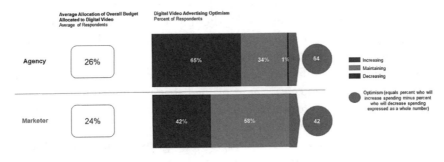

Figure 24.4 A slide from "The Future of Digital Video" by Trusted Media Brands Inc.

The survey may also tie findings to Trusted Media Brands' business. For example, this same survey asked respondents if Trusted Media Brands is a publisher "providing trusted, brand-safe environments for digital advertising."

The content is gated on a landing page, so users enter their basic information. This method allows Trusted Media Brands to track usage.

The Museum at Eldridge Street

So far, we have looked at consumer and B2B for-profit companies. Now, let's turn to a nonprofit museum located in New York City's historic Lower East Side.

The Museum at Eldridge Street is separate from the Eldridge Street Synagogue. The synagogue itself was erected in 1887 and is called the "first immigrant-built synagogue in the United States." In the early 20th century, the synagogue was well known for its celebrity cantors, its magnificent architecture, and its respite from the crowded streets of what was then the most crowded neighborhood in the world. Though once a prominent synagogue during the immigration boom during the early decades of the 1900s, by the 1950s things had changed. The main sanctuary was not used from 1955 to 1980 and fell into disrepair. In the early 1970s, a professor at New York University discovered the decrepit interior. Over the ensuing the decades, the historic sanctuary was restored. It took 20 years and about $20 million. Most of the sanctuary is original, including the floors and chandeliers.

The Museum at Eldridge tells the story of the synagogue's history and the larger history of immigration. Executive Director Bonnie Dimun notes, "This is the story of all new immigrant groups who come to a new land and try to retain some cultural elements."[14] The museum communicates this story through synagogue exhibits, tours, events, concerts, festivals, neighborhood walking tours, and educational programming.

Amy Stein-Milford, former deputy director, offered great insight into the museum's content strategies. She explained that the museum uses content marketing to increase registration for group tours, individual tours, events, and rentals for private events.

On the museum's website, Eldridgestreet.org, users can register for any of these tours and events. The museum plans to further enhance the site by sharing video highlights from key events. There will be interviews with scholars or other presenters on the museum's website, YouTube channel, and its social media channels.

Event promotion

Events are a primary way the museum engages participants, donors, tourists, and locals. The museum provides an assortment of events including building tours, after-hours events, walking tours, talks and lectures, concerts, and family events.

Multicultural festivals have proven to be the most popular events, attracting a large number of young adults and their families. The most well known is the Egg Roll, Egg Cream, and Empanada Festival, which presents music, food, theater, cooking, and talks from the Chinese, Latino (Puerto Rican and Dominican), and Jewish cultures.

There is also a synchronicity between online and off-line engagement. At events, signs and announcements encourage attendees to take pictures and share them on social media sites such as Facebook and the visual-oriented Instagram. Visitors' photos, when shared, are then posted on the museum's Pinterest page under the section "Photos by Our Visitors." On the museum's social media sites, staff post pictures and videos of events and extended content related to event themes and promote future events.

The museum also engages online users through timely and engaging blogs. Encompassing a variety of voices, the blogs include stories from the woman who runs the front desk, volunteers, curators, and others. The "Friday of Eldridge Street" highlights someone with a special connection to Eldridge Street such as longtime volunteers. Some articles are humorous. Each article

Figure 24.5 Restored interior of Eldridge Street Synagogue. Photograph by Kate Milford. Courtesy of The Museum at Eldridge Street.

is also posted on Facebook. Other blogs are extensions of exhibit content. For example, the blog for the exhibit *Lost Synagogues of Europe* explored the current status and histories of synagogues featured in the collection. It focused on the few that have been preserved. Then, the blog linked that to the museum's overall mission of restoring and preserving.

To promote these events, the museum uses a number of channels:

- Sends out event press releases to a targeted list. The PR list has close to 1,000 names, but each event is promoted to a small, select group.

- Deploys event emails to anywhere between 1,000 and 12,000 people depending on the event.

- Lists all events in the monthly email, which goes out to 14,000.

The museum has about 20,000 on its email list, which is segmented into different lists for microtargeting, including monthly email only, adult learners, concert attendees, press, donors, families, and more.

The mailing list has thousands of names, but typically the museum promotes only to the most recent donors (people who have donated in the last two or three years), museum visitors event attendees, and other special interest groups.

Stein-Milford reflected on the efficacy of each channel: "We find mail still important for our donors who are older but less and less important for our program attendees. The email list and single-event emails have very good response for us. We also use social media to get the word out, including Facebook, Twitter, and Instagram. On Facebook, we do boosted posts. Instagram is used more to encourage visitors to share their experience following their visit."

The museum also tracks the cost-benefits for each channel. The most costly is direct mail, with the caveat that a subsection of older donors is responsive to this medium. The next is social media and then email. Partnerships are another way for the museum to promote events.

Stein-Milford explained the importance of partnering: "The right partner can be very helpful in both planning and promoting the event. Other partners we've found less effective and so we have been more strategic about who we team up with, and have tried to involve them earlier on so it is a true collaboration and both organizations are invested in the success of the event."

The museum has experienced success with third-party sites for promoting some key events. For example, Untapped Cities, Brooklyn Brainery, and Atlas Obscura are all organizations that present unique sites and experiences in New York City and beyond and also reach a younger audience. For tours, the museum partners with third-party organizations such as New York Pass and Smartsave.

Stein-Milford also commented on the importance of third-party travel review sites: "Travel review sites like TripAdvisor and Yelp are hugely influential in getting the word out. We are also putting in place the sale of tickets through online ticketing organizations like Viator, which is connected to Trip Advisor. After people read our reviews, which are quite positive, they will immediately be able to book their tour ticket."

Soliciting feedback

The museum solicits feedback formally through program and tour surveys distributed at select programs. They also conduct email surveys following major events such as the Egg Rolls, Egg Creams & Empanadas Festival, Jane Jacobs talks, and other prominent events.

Stein-Milford noted that she is "curious in hearing more from the people who have not yet made it to the museum. 'Why haven't they made it here? How do they perceive us? What has stopped them from coming here.' That is a goal for the future but a much harder group to reach."

Reaching a younger demographic

Demographically, the museum targets varies segments. Its audience for concerts and talks tends to be older. While the museum aims to grow this segment, it also wants to attract young adults (20s and 30s) and families with young children to its programming.

The museum conducted a focus group with its targeted audience. Amy explained the key findings: "We found that traditional marketing of old is not how young people hear about events. They predominately hear of events through word of mouth and recommendations through friends, so social media and enlisting younger ambassadors is essential. Also, they are looking for sites and activities that have cultural and social resonance. They are not just looking for an activity with beer included. Rather they want to learn something and contribute. There are a number of activities that we offer that speak directly to this and we have to do a better job of communicating this when promoting our events to the millennial audience."

Final Words

I hope this book has inspired you to create and bring to market content. Perhaps it has encouraged you to leverage the thought leaders in your organization. Or maybe it has egged you on to build a robust campaign management system or to enable your sales team. If there's one takeaway, it's that content marketing can transform how your brand is viewed in the marketplace and how you capture, nurture, and close leads.

Now, create great content and put it to work.

Notes

Chapter 1, "What Content Marketing Can Do for You"

1. https://contentmarketinginstitute.com/what-is-content-marketing/.

2. "The Sophisticated Marketer's Guide to Thought Management," LinkedIn Marketing Solutions, https://business.linkedin.com/content/dam/business/marketing-solutions/global/en_US/campaigns/pdfs/sophisticated-guide-thought-leadership.pdf.

3. Ibid.

4. http://blog.eloqua.com/thought-leadership-marketing/.

5. SAVO, "Techniques of Social Selling: Just Do It!," 2014, http://www.slideshare.net/SAVO_Group/techniques-of-social-selling-just-do-it-sales-for-life.

6. "The Sophisticated Marketer's Guide to Thought Management," LinkedIn Marketing Solutions, https://business.linkedin.com/content/dam/business/marketing-solutions/global/en_US/campaigns/pdfs/sophisticated-guide-thought-leadership.pdf.

7. https://www.bloomgroup.com/blogs/tim-parker/content-marketing-vs-thought-leadership-marketing-difference-twixt-two.

8. https://www.bloomgroup.com/content/competing-thought-leadership-seven-hallmarks-compelling-intellectual-capital-0.

Chapter 2, "Creating Your Content Marketing Plan"

1. https://www.smartinsights.com/online-pr/online-pr-outreach/types-of-influencers.

Chapter 6, "Best Practices in Content Development"

1. ITSMA, "2016 How B2B Buyers Consume Information and Content During the Buying Process Study."

2. Ibid.

3. https://www.cebglobal.com/marketing-communications/digital-evolution.html.

4. https://www.bloomgroup.com/content/best-practitioners-offer-four-best-practices-thought-leadership.

5. Ibid.

Chapter 7, "Pitfalls in Choosing a Topic"

1. https://www.bloomgroup.com/blogs/bob-buday/how-choose-right-research-topic-your-next-thought-leadership-study.

2. https://www.bloomgroup.com.

3. Ibid.

Chapter 8, "Editorial Project Planning"

1. Pam Didner, *Global Content Marketing* (New York: McGraw-Hill, 2015), 108.

Chapter 12, "Building a Campaign Landing Page"

1. David Cummings and Adam Blitzer, *Think Outside the Inbox: The B2B Automation Guide* (Atlanta, GA: Leigh Walker Books, 2010), 118.

Chapter 13, "Troubleshooting Landing Pages"

1. https://demandbase.com.

Chapter 15, "Social Media"

1. Brian Halligan and Dharmesh Shah, *Inbound Marketing: Attract, Engage, and Delight Customers Online* (New York: Wiley, 2014).

2. https://twitter.com.

3. https://zephoria.com/top-15-valuable-facebook-statistics and Source: State of Inbound Marketing 2012

4. http://www.digitalmarketer.com/youtube-ad-types.

5. Halligan and Shah, *Inbound Marketing: Attract, Engage, and Delight Customers Online*, 92.

Chapter 16, "Pay-Per-Click Advertising"

1. https://support.google.com.

2. http://www.dasdm.com.

Chapter 17, "Organic Search Results"

1. Halligan and Shah, *Inbound Marketing: Attract, Engage, and Delight Customers Online*, 47.

2. Ibid.

3. Ibid.

Chapter 19, "Lead Nurturing"

1. Paul McFedries, *Word Spy: The Word Lover's Guide to Modern Culture* (New York: Broadway Books, 2004), 90.

2. Lori Feldman, guest blogger, "Nine Must Have Drip Campaigns," https://community.act.com/t5/The-Act-Journal/Nine-Must-Have-Drip-Marketing-Campaigns-Guest-Blog-by-Lori/ba-p/57345.

Chapter 20, "Sales and Marketing Systems"

1. Cummings and Blitzer, *Think Outside the Inbox: The B2B Automation Guide*, referencing a 2009 Forrester Research study.

2. Halligan and Shah, *Inbound Marketing: Attract, Engage, and Delight Customers Online*, 139.

Chapter 21, "How Thought Leadership Helps Sales"

1. Huanhuan Shi, Shrihari Sridhar, Rajdeep Grewal, and Gary Lilien, "Sales Representative Departures and Customer Reassignment Strategies in Business-to-Business Markets." *Journal of Marketing* 81, no. 2 (March 2017): 25–44.

Chapter 24, "Profiles"

1. https://www.digitalistmag.com/customer-experience/2017/01/20/best-content-marketing-examples-04835767.

2. https://marketinginsidergroup.com/content-marketing/open-forum-gold-standard-content-marketing.

3. Ibid.

4. Ibid.

5. https://contently.com/strategist/2016/04/13/3-content-marketing-takeaways-american-express.

6. http://solutionsinsights.com/role-thought-leadership-marketing-solutions-ibm.

7. Ibid.

8. https://www.itsma.com/using-thought-leadership-stand-sea-sameness.

9. Ibid.

10. Ibid.

11. https://linkhumans.com/blog/whole-foods.

12. http://www.epicbrandz.com/brand-reviews/whole-foods/why-whole-foods-market-wins-big-when-it-comes-to-content-marketing.

13. http://tmbi.com/trusted-media-brands-survey-reports-now-ever-marketers-need-targeted-brand-safe-environments/.

14. Paul Kaplan, *Jewish New York: A History and Guide to Neighborhoods, Synagogues, and Eateries* (New Orleans, LA: Pelican Publishing, 2015).

Glossary

A/B Testing: Testing of multiple versions in a campaign to see which yields the best result. In its simplest form, all variables are held constant except one.

Bidding Software: Tools that allow users to optimize their bidding strategies for their paid search efforts. These tools work across search engines and seek to obtain the best search ranking for the lowest cost per click.

Buyer's Funnel: The classic stages a typical buyer goes through in making a purchase decision. Typical stages are awareness, familiarity, consideration, purchase, and loyalty.

Closed Sale: More typically used in large B2B transactions, the completed purchase of service or product denoted by a signed contract and initial payment.

Content Management Tools: Software that allows users to add, edit, and provide basic functionality to a website. Current industry leaders are Drupal and SquareSpace are two examples.

Conversion: A desired action that a user took such as downloaded content, attended a webinar, registered for an event, or requested a demo. Each campaign needs to define what the conversion action is.

Customer Relationship Management (CRM): Strategies and tools companies employ to manage and analyze customer and prospect interactions at various contact points and across channels. Salesforce is currently one of the leading CRM tools.

Dedupe: The elimination of duplicative records when merging two lists.

Gated Content: Exclusive content on a website for which users must enter contact information or other demographic information in order to access

Hard Bounce: An email with a failed delivery usually because the recipient's address is not valid or the domain name doesn't exist.

Hero Image: A prominent, large banner image placed front and center on a web page. Usually, it is what the visitor sees first so its content plays a very important role.

Marketing Automation Tools: Software to execute campaigns like emails and social media and to score, grade, and route leads. Often marketing automation tools are synchronized with a CRM tool. Industry leaders include Eloqua and Marketo.

Operational Metrics: In the content of digital marketing campaigns, these are performance numbers showing more detailed metrics, usually for campaign owners rather than for senior management. Examples include delivery rates, unsubscribe rates, open rates, click-through rates, like/share/comment/retweets, page traffic, and time on site.

Persona: A fictional character who represents the key characteristics of a group of users for whom to customize an online journey. Examples include HR Manager, Facilities Director, or Procurement Director.

Scorecard: A series of metrics to showcase the performance of a marketing campaign, usually updated regularly and shared with senior management.

Search Engine Marketing (SEM): Optimizing bids, keywords, and copy to solicit website traffic through buying ads on search engines. SEM campaigns should always have a defined goal or conversion metric.

Search Engine Optimization (SEO): Improving the organic ranking on a search display page (Google, Bing, Yahoo etc.) to a website through optimizing copy, keywords, link equity, and technical improvements allowing for efficient web crawls. The goal is ultimately to increase web page traffic and conversions.

Soft Bounce: An email that reaches the recipient's mail server but bounces back as undelivered, usually because the recipient's mailbox is full or set for "out of office" and not receiving incoming messages.

Web Analytics Tools: The measurement and analysis of web data including page traffic, sources, user engagement metrics, and conversion data for optimizing web usage.

References

Books
Anand, Bharat, *Content Trap*. New York: Random House, 2016.

Cummings, David and Adam Blitzer, *Think Outside the Inbox: The B2B Marketing Automation Guide*. Atlanta, GA: Leigh Walker Books, 2010.

Didner, Pam, *Global Content*. New York: McGraw-Hill Education, 2015.

Halligan, Brian and Shah Dharmesh, *Inbound Marketing: Attract, Engage, and Delight Customers Online*. New York: Wiley, 2014.

Halvorson, Kristina and Melissa Rach, *Content Strategy for the Web*. New York: New Riders, 2012.

Journals
Shi, Huanhuan, Sridhar, Shrihari, Grewal, Rajdeep, and Lilien, Gary (2017) "Sales Representative Departures and Customer Reassignment Strategies in Business-to-Business Markets." *Journal of Marketing*: March 2017, Vol. 81, No. 2, pp. 25-44.

Online Resources
LinkedIn Marketing Solutions, "The Sophisticated Marketer's Guide to Content Marketing, downloaded from business.linkedin.com/marketing-solutions/marketing-strategy

Forrester Research, "Nurture Thought Leadership to Nurture Your Brand," April 2013.

Websites
Act.com blog, Lori Feldman, guest blogger, "Nine Must Have Drip Campaigns"

Americanexpress.com/us/small-business/openforum/explore

Aytm.com/blog/research-junction/top-50-brands-using-content-marketing-with-positive-results
Bloomgroup.com
Contently.com/strategist/2016/04/13/3-content-marketing-takeaways-american-express
CEBGlobal.com, site for Corporate Executive Board
Demandbase.com
D!gitialistMagazine.com
Digitalmarketer.com/youtube-ad-types
Epicbrandz.com/brand-reviews/whole-foods/why-whole-foods-market-wins-big-when-it-comes-to-content-marketing
Itsma.com
Linkedin.com
Linkhumans.com/blog/whole-foods
Marketinginsidergroup.com/content-marketing/open-forum-gold-standard-content-marketing
Solutionsinsights.com/role-thought-leadership-marketing-solutions-ibm
Support.google.com
TMBI.org
Twitter.com

Interviews

Rob Leavitt, Senior Vice President, Thought Leadership Practice, ITSMA, Boston, Massachusetts
Tim Parker, Partner, Bloom Group, Boston, Massachusetts
Amy Stein Milford, Deputy Director, Museum at Eldridge Street, New York
Rich Sutton, Chief Revenue Office, Trusted Media Brands, Incorporated (formerly, Reader's Digest Association), New York, NY

Organizations' Content—Used with Permission

Bloom Group blogs
ITSMA, 2016 How B2B Buyers Consume Information and Content during the Buying Process Study
Heinz Marketing, The Modern Marketer's Workshop, Content that Converts, heinzmarketing.com
SmartInsights.com infographic

Index

About the Author

PAUL KAPLAN writes books in three categories: cultural guides; social history & biographies; and business marketing. His other six books include *New York's Original Penn Station: The Rise and Fall of an American Landmark*; *Lillian Wald: America's Great Social & Healthcare Reformer*; *Progressive Era (1890–1920) in New York*; *Irving Berlin: The Story Behind the Composer of White Christmas & God Bless America*; *Jewish New York: A History & Guide to Neighborhoods, Synagogues, and Eateries* and a sequel for South Florida.

He has been featured on CBS Miami, WNET/PBS, the front page of *New York Press*, the iconic African-American newspaper *Amsterdam New York*, *Princeton Magazine* and nationally-airing radio shows including *America's Dining & Travel*, *Writer's Voice*, *Let's Travel* and *Woodstock Booktalk with Martha Frankel*.

He has given over 40 talks at venues across the US including the Harvard Club, Yale Club, Union League of New York, General Society Library, New York Public Library, Museum at Eldridge Street, Miami Design Preservation League, and to corporations, schools, community centers and private events.

He earned a BA in Ethics, Politics, and Economics from Yale College and an MBA from Yale School of Management. Kaplan has worked in marketing for over 15 years focused on content marketing/thought leadership, digital media and product strategy for educational technology and financial companies. He has served in senior marketing roles at Princeton Review-Tutor.com, American Express, McGraw-Hill and Broadridge Financial Solutions. He has performed many consulting engagements on marketing strategy and execution.